G000124314

THE CHURCH THAT
JESUS BUILT

THE CHURCH THAT JESUS BUILT

All content enquiries to cleland@clelandthom.co.uk

First published 2021

Published by Quest Publications
questpublications@outlook.com

Cover image - Copyright: Stockcreations

ISBN-13: 978-1-988439-33-4

By the Same Author

MOSES, THE MAKING OF A LEADER. Published by Kingsway in the UK and Victory Press in America. Book of the Day at Spring Harvest.

ABRAHAM, FRIEND OF GOD. Published by Kingsway.

BROKEN-HEARTED BELIEVERS. Published by Kingsway in the UK and Karas Sana in Finland.

FRIENDS OF GOD. Co-written with Jeff Lucas. Published by Crossway.

THE POWER TO PERSUADE. Published by Pioneer.

DESTINY CALLS, first edition. Published by Canaan Press. Ghost-written for Norman and Grace Barnes.

QUESTIONABLE SUPERNATURAL. Published by Amazon.

DESTINY CALLS, second edition. Published by Clean Copy Editing. Written with Norman and Grace Barnes.

THE PATH OF THE SEER. Published by Amazon.

DONATIONS

I do not make any money from my books, podcasts, or resources.

Anything you paid for this book covers Amazon's fees. All other income goes to Rays of Sunshine Home for Abused and Abandoned babies, near Cape Town, South Africa.

You can donate here:

https://www.paypal.com/paypalme/rayofsunshinehouse

DEDICATION

This book is dedicated to my dear friends, Keith and Carole Berkley.

Their lives are an inspiration to me and so many others.

And their friendship, love and wisdom mean more to me than I can describe.

CONTENTS

PREFACE

When I was at school, we played a game called Opposites.

Whatever the teacher did, we did the opposite. So, if she raised her right hand, we raised our left.

She said it developed coordination. For me, it developed confusion!

The Christian church has been playing Opposites with Jesus for hundreds of years.

Jesus said: 'Go and make disciples.' But we stay and make converts.

He said: 'Cast out demons.' But we train counsellors.

He said: 'Do not exalt yourself.' But we gather Facebook followers.

He also said: 'I will build my church.' But we have frequently built it ourselves.

And look what's happened.

COVID-19 exposed the church's poverty of power.

But Jesus *will* build his church. It will be powerful and passionate, ridiculously reckless and utterly unpredictable. It will expose our DIY versions as grotesque parodies.

Only churches that Jesus builds will survive in the end times. If that excites you, join me in discovering what they can be like.

Cleland Thom

Chichester, 2021.

Chapter 1

So, WHOSE CHURCH IS IT ANYWAY?

I t's hard to find Jesus in some churches.

I visited a large, respected church before the COVID-19 lockdown, and he wasn't mentioned. Not in the songs, not in the talk, not in words of prophecy or encouragement. And not in any bible readings, because there weren't any.

So, in truth, it wasn't really a church. It was just a group of people doing religious things, as you can't have a church without Jesus.

No wonder God put us into lockdown. He wanted people to discover Jesus for themselves, at home.

It's hard to find Jesus on church websites, too.

Some of the country's most 'significant' churches, streams and denominations scarcely mention him. Many ignore him completely.

One 'church' that preached salvation by grace buried him on their legal page!

Does your church's website pass the Where's Jesus test? Take a look. You might be surprised.

But in some ways, it makes sense. Many churches are built by people. So, why would they honour Jesus? Instead, they honour the men and women who built them.

Where have YOU buried him?

If you bury Jesus, you side with Satan. He hates the name of Jesus, too. It makes his demons tremble, and he'll do anything to keep him under wraps.

Some churches pass Jesus off as 'the Christ', which he certainly is. But he is Jesus, the head of the church, the author and finisher of our faith, the name above every other name.

He is the only name by which people can be saved. He is the way, the truth and the life. He is the only way to the Father.

Some churches bury Jesus because they fear offending people. So, they avoid 'speaking out boldly in the name of the Lord' (Acts 9:28) and keep the good news secret.

But churches that don't exalt the name of Jesus eventually die. That's why many church buildings are now used for everything from mosques to Mecca bingo, and why many newer churches have folded up.

They were Jesus-deniers.

Jesus said in Matthew 10:33: 'Everyone who denies me here on earth, I will also deny before my Father in heaven.'

So, if a church denies Jesus, he will deny them before his Father. Dangerous territory. Yet many churches are more afraid of denying climate change than denying Jesus.

And speaking of climate change, the Archbishop of Canterbury didn't mention him either in his recent statement.

He stuck to 'God' ... a bit safer.

If he won't mention Jesus, who will?

Maybe me and you.

With a vision, people perish

I once went to a church's annual meeting, and the leader outlined the church's vision.

Again, he didn't mention Jesus.

I thought this was strange, as Jesus said in Matthew 16:18 that **he** would build his church. So, you think he'd warrant a mention.

Instead, the leader spoke about himself, his apostle, his leadership team and the churches he had planted.

3

He showed graphs, projections and plans. But he didn't refer to the builder.

He was a Jesus denier, too.

Sadly, this episode wasn't unusual. Many churches have a 'vision'.

They take the verse 'without a vision, people perish' (Proverbs 29:18) out of context and use it justify secular vision building.

Eventually, the vision predominates. And people perish, because it is Jesus, not the vision, who sustains all things by his powerful word (Hebrews 1:3). He holds things together (Colossians 1:17).

Adding other things to Jesus is sometimes called Jesus-plus.

It's nothing new. In the past, there's been Jesus-plus-baptism, Jesus-plus-the-gifts-of-the-Spirit, Jesus-plus-music.

But Jesus-**plus** something equals **nothing**. He stands supreme. He won't share his glory or headship with anyone.

Hebrews 12:2 invites us to fix our eyes on Jesus, the pioneer and perfecter of faith. In Aramaic, the language Jesus used, *fixing* also means: 'Looking away from everything else.'

4

So, we must look **away** from our church's vision and gaze on him and his beauty while he builds the church. He's good at it if we give him the chance.

The first church in Jerusalem didn't have a vision. They had a commission. That should be enough for us, too.

So, what's a church?

Jesus only mentioned the word *church* twice during his time on earth. And both times, the bible uses the Greek word *ekklesia,* which means 'a gathering of called out ones'.

So, Jesus was referring to people, not a building like a synagogue.

And when he referred to 'church', it didn't exist, so he used a visual aid.

A few years earlier, he invited 12 men to gather round him. They were the first church.

To some, he just said: 'Follow me.' No compulsion, no pressure. Take it or leave it. No zero-hours contract or a part-time deal. It was all or nothing. They had to leave everything, especially their worldly values and thinking.

And three years later, he reported back his Father in John 17: 'They are not of the world, even as I am not of it.' Job done. This was fundamental to discipleship.

5

It still is.

The world, the flesh and the deism

1 John 2:15 tells us not to love the world or anything in it.

But many churches love the world so much they have become just like it. They are playing with fire. Remember, Satan is still the prince of the world, despite Jesus' victory on the cross. 1 John 5:19 says: 'The whole world is under the control of the evil one.'

Jesus recognised Satan's title in John 14.30: 'I will not say much more to you, for the prince of this world is coming.'

So, any church that is controlled by worldly systems, values and procedures risks handing power to the prince.

Here's a good test. How many of these does your church use?

- Charity status
- Bank accounts
- Trusts
- Public buildings
- Secular administrative and leadership structures

- Policies and procedures for things like data protection, child protection, diversity and privacy.

Then ask: could your church function without them?

If the answer is 'No', then perhaps you depend more on Satan's tools more than the Holy Spirit and the word of God. As a result, your church will be powerless and will be reluctant to use the name of Jesus publicly.

James 4:4 calls this spiritual adultery: 'You adulterous people, don't you know that friendship with the world means enmity against God? Therefore, anyone who chooses to be a friend of the world becomes an enemy of God.'

Jesus' best friend John, added in 1 John 2:15 that God's love is **not even in us** if we befriend the world. Ouch!

This doesn't mean that we should not use secular tools. Of course, we should. But we need to ask ourselves whether they control us.

So, maybe ask yourself another question. If your church didn't have the items on the list above, what would be left?

Your answer may be: 'Just people and God.' And that's probably how he wants it.

Father God loves to dwell with his people (Exodus 29:45), not with their buildings, their structures or their systems.

Set in stones

In bible days, builders laid the cornerstone, or foundation stone, on a new building first. Then they fitted the other stones round it.

So, if the cornerstone wasn't perfectly aligned, every other stone would be off-centre, and the building would eventually collapse.

God sent Jesus as our cornerstone. Isaiah 28:16 says: 'Behold, I am laying in Zion a stone, a tested stone, a costly cornerstone for the foundation, firmly placed.' Peter later confirmed this (1 Peter 2:4-7).

So, if we build churches with a secular cornerstone, then every living stone - that's me and you - will be out of line. And the church won't last.

A pandemic of worldliness

COVID-19 was God's building inspection.

He gave churches the chance to repent of depending on the prince of this world and to rebuild, using Jesus as their cornerstone.

Some responded. But many were hungry to 'get back to normal' and are now befriending the prince's world once again.

Society has had enough 'normal'. God's word promises **supernormal**. The dictionary defines this as: 'Beyond the range of the normal or scientifically explainable.'

That should be our goal. Otherwise, we're a religious social club.

Council culture

When Jesus talked about church, he didn't use the Greek word *ekklesia*, but the Aramaic word *edata*, which means a *body of believers*.

Now, *edata* comes from the Aramaic root word *eta*, which means *a town council*.

So, Jesus was referring to *people with a governing function*.

And he demonstrated this by bringing his government to a world suffering from sickness, demons, injustice, sin and religion, as Isaiah prophesied (Isaiah 9:6).

Edata also mirrors the Old Testament leadership style, where Moses appointed elders to judge groups of 100s, 50s and 10s (Exodus 18:25).

So, the church that Jesus built with his 12 disciples was a gathering of believers who had responded to his call to be with him.

They separated themselves from the world and their old lives.

And they were 'governed' by an authority figure ... Jesus, a foot washing servant who was willing to die for them.

Jesus was from an ordinary background. He had another job. In Mark 6:3 people asked: 'Isn't this the carpenter?' Note the present tense. He still worked for a living.

He was a man of the people, who queued up to get baptised by his cousin John (Luke 3:21).

He was holy, but not haughty. He loved the poor, the needy, the outcasts, the sick and the demonised.

Sinners loved him because he loved them. Yet he remained pure among prostitutes and untainted by tax collectors.

He governed his followers, sickness, the devil, the weather and the elements with extraordinary supernatural power.

His group didn't have a name, just a reputation. It was radical, not religious.

It was governed by compassion, not a constitution, love instead of legalism and power instead of performance. It had miracles instead of membership and deliverance instead of a denomination.

It was inclusive and exclusive.

Jesus discouraged some people from joining (Mark 10:17-22) and gave those in it the opportunity to leave (John 6:67).

Time to go ...

After Jesus ascended to be with his Father, the 11 remaining disciples were unequipped to build a church and thankfully, they didn't try to.

They just took Matthias off the subs' bench and waited for the power of the Spirit to replicate Jesus' church in Jerusalem.

Thousands responded to Peter's invitation to be 'called out'.

They left everything and gathered under the servant leadership of the 12 apostles, who like Jesus, provided spiritual government.

Edata.

Fast forward, not pause

2021 years later, there are thousands of cultural expressions of church across the globe. Some are calm, some are chaotic. Some peaceful, some powerful. Some loving, some legalistic.

They're all affected by sin, deception, division and failure, although some are better at hiding it than others.

And Jesus is still calling people to have their hearts circumcised by the Holy Spirit and leave everything to follow him.

He is still looking for 11 people plus one substitute - that's me or you - who will separate themselves from the world to be with him.

He is not looking for religion, organisations or buildings. Our world has enough of them already.

He wants to build his church. His way. But sometimes he must uproot and tear down, to destroy and overthrow before he can build and plant (Jeremiah 1:10).

Wave goodbye

In December 2018, God warned me that he was sending a wave of judgement to destroy 'manufactured' church structures.

He told me to publish it after the Indonesian tsunami.

He said: 'I am calling my church to rise and begin to reverse this country's political, moral and social decline.

'But judgement must start with the house of God (1 Peter 4:19).

'Jeremiah 51:42 says: "The sea will rise over Babylon; she will sink under its roaring waves."

'I will release a tidal wave of judgement upon the church unless it repents of the compromises that have given power to the spirit of Babylon.

'Churches that don't heed me will lose their funds, or their buildings, or both. Others will be swept away because I did not build them' (Psalm 127:1).

'Entire movements and organisations, even those that appear strong and significant both nationally and internationally, will discover that they were built on sand (Matthew 7:26-27) and collapse.

'My wave will shake church structures, to reveal what was built by me, and what was built by human hands (Hebrews 12:26-27).

'Churches that have dug their own cisterns (Jeremiah 2:13), using secular structures, will collapse like buildings in a tsunami.

'I will tear down leadership hierarchies and exalt true servants to lead my people. I alone will cover them.

'I will demolish the Babylonian system of accountability and set my people free to become the church that Jesus builds.

'My wave will expose every compromise with the new age, the occult and other gods.

'I will wash away worship led through human effort by those with uncircumcised hearts (Philippians 3:3) and exalt those who worship in Spirit and in truth (John 4:24).

'There is time to repent. The kingdom of heaven **is** at hand, and Jesus will build his church for your nation's sake.'

That prophecy came true and is still coming true.

The wave was COVID-19. Significantly, the government referred to it as a 'wave'. And when the virus struck, many Christians missed the point and responded by recording the Blessing Song.

It was a nice song with biblical words and encouraged a lot of people.

But it also perpetuated the problem. God's anger is not soothed with a singsong.

He was calling his people to humble themselves and cry out for mercy. He still is.

Another warning

In May 2020, God gave me another word for the church, a few months before the second wave of COVID-19 began.

He said: 'I am angry because my people have set aside my laws and worshipped other gods. Many have ignored my call to repent.

'So, I will bring a second wave of judgement that will be more terrible than the first.

'I used the COVID-19 lockdown to lead those with ears to hear out of the "Egypt" in their hearts and in their churches.

'These saints are now at the border of a Promised Land and must decide whether to go in and possess it.

'But churches that try to return to Business as Usual will find that the Holy Spirit has moved on. "Church" as they knew it is finished and if they try to resurrect it, they will labour in vain.

'Those who put buildings ahead of living stones will gradually disappear.

'And those who have rendered to Caesar instead of rendering to God will reap what they have sown.

'I have my winnowing fork in my hand and will clear the threshing floor of compromise.

'I will soon require each believer and each congregation to choose between the broad road of compromise or the narrow path of my word.

'Many will have to take agonising decisions because of their compromises. The consequences will be astonishing and shocking.

'But if you repent now, it will be easier later.

'Many have already allowed the enemy to start engraving his mark on their hearts and will find it acceptable to take his mark on their bodies later.

'I am inviting you to search your hearts, confess your sin, and repent. My arms of love and mercy are still open wide.'

You won't miss the boat

Up to now, churches have been like boats. Manufactured. Safe and structured. But many sank in the COVID-19 storm. Others are sinking.

So now, we must learn to walk on water and look to Jesus, not to the prince of this world, with his systems, procedures, policies and structures.

It will be stormy and supernatural. But, if you begin to sink, Jesus will catch you.

Battering or buttering?

Jesus first described his church as a battering ram.

He said: 'I will build my church, and the gates of hell shall not prevail against it.' He was describing a siege, where attackers battered down a city's gates.

Is your church a battering ram, or just butter and jam at the next church social?

If Jesus builds it, it will batter enemy strongholds, whatever its mission.

But if you build it, it will be butter and jam - sweet and tasty, but bad for your health, especially your heart.

Before Jesus returned to his Father, he told his disciples to preach the gospel to all creation.

And in Mark 16:17-19 he added it would be a supernatural mission. Believers would speak in tongues and do miracles. They would conflict with demons and sickness.

That's why around 25 per cent of his mission involved deliverance. Another 25 per cent involved healing. Does yours?

Any church that Jesus builds will be in a constant war against sickness, idolatry, poverty, injustice and religion.

It will be unafraid to say that Jesus is the only way to the Father.

It will be chaotic and unstoppable. It will be a warrior church of love.

In contrast, 'butter and jam' churches are religious social clubs.

Their gospel is so diluted, it's not worth having. They have a form of godliness but are devoid of any power (2 Timothy 3:5).

There is little to separate them from an organisation called the Sunday Assembly, where people gather to sing songs, hear moving stories, listen to passionate speakers and enjoy friendship, coffee and donuts.

It says that attenders will be 'energised, revitalised, restored, repaired, refreshed and recharged'.

But it's secular. It has nothing to do with God. However, their meetings are like many pre-lockdown Christian services.

No wonder God closed them for 18 months. He was inviting them to let Jesus to take over.

And they face a difficult future if they decide to go back to normal.

The enemy wants us to conform to the world, to be friends of the world, and to be so lovingly nice that we have the cutting edge of a bowl of custard.

If you want to be culturally relevant, the church that Jesus builds may not the place for you.

The church that Jesus builds will provide what the world can't.

Chapter 2

POWER ON PURPOSE

The church that Jesus built was powerful. That's what caught people's attention. Jesus and his disciples performed hundreds of miracles during three dynamic years.

Dr Luke explained in Acts 10:38: 'He went around doing good and healing all who were under the power of the devil, because God was with him.'

Jesus cleansed lepers, healed diseases and deformities and set people free from demons.

Then, when he returned to heaven, the church in Jerusalem carried on where he left off.

So should we. Any church that is not supernatural is superficial.

This is why Paul said: 'My message and my preaching were not with wise and persuasive words, but with a demonstration of the Spirit's power.'

The COVID-19 pandemic exposed the church's power vacuum.

Revelation 3:17 sums up our impotence: 'You say, "I am rich; I have acquired wealth and do not need a thing." But you do not realise that you are wretched, pitiful, poor, blind and naked.'

Promises rewritten

I believe Father God is angry at the way Christians have treated his precious healing promises.

Many people deny he heals at all, while others have turned healing into a mind-over-matter 'confess' formula.

Some have used healing to achieve fame and finance or have made it mystic by compromising with the new age and the occult.

Others have turned it to a tick-box method or added godless methods of inner healing or ridiculous behaviour that they attribute the Holy Spirit.

It is very difficult to find anyone who heals the way Jesus did.

Then we wonder why healings are rare. We must get back to the maker's instructions. They work!

God's first healing sermon

In Exodus 15:26, the Israelites had just witnessed God part the Red Sea and defeat the Egyptian armies.

But the novelty soon wore off. Three days later they were stuck in the wilderness without water.

The best that Moses could find was bitter water at Marah. So, the Israelites started grumbling. They had forgotten the last miracle and didn't have faith for the next one.

Then, God said to the Israelites: 'If you listen carefully to the LORD your God and do what is right in his eyes, if you pay attention to his commands and keep all his decrees, I will not bring on you any of the diseases I brought on the Egyptians, for I am the LORD, who heals you.'

So, he revealed himself as the healer in just 52 words. And he included two **ifs** and two key points.

A conditional covenant

First, he said healing was conditional on obedience. For Christians, it still is. Many miss this and remain sick.

God sent Jesus to offer a new covenant of salvation, healing and forgiveness. But like any covenant, both sides have a part to play.

1 Peter 2:24 sets out God's side with regards to healing: 'Jesus bore our sins in his body on the cross and by his wounds you have been healed.'

Matthew 8:16-17 confirms that this verse applies to physical healing and deliverance. It says: 'When evening came, many who were demon-possessed were brought to him, and he drove out the spirits with a word and healed all the sick.

'This was to fulfil what was spoken through the prophet Isaiah: "He took up our infirmities and bore our diseases."'

Our part is to confess and believe (Romans 10:9).

But God also knows that we sin and get things wrong. So, he invites us to have a spiritual health check every time we take communion.

This is so important. Churches that don't break bread a lot usually sin a lot. And the congregation gets sick a lot.

Paul says in 1 Corinthians 11:27-31 that if we break bread in an unworthy manner, we sin against the body and blood of the Lord. These are the elements of the covenant.

And he adds: 'Those who eat and drink without discerning the body of Christ eat and drink judgement on themselves. That is why many among you are weak and sick, and a number of you have fallen asleep.'

So, for a Christian, communion is either a blessing or a curse. We either confirm our side of God's covenant and should remain healthy. Or we ignore the conditions and may become sick.

Now, I'm not saying that all sickness is due to sin. We live in a disease-ridden world. Our bodies decay as we get older. And some sicknesses don't have an identifiable cause.

But personally, if I'm ill, I examine my heart, as Paul advises. It's the best place to start.

God sets other conditions, too.

James 5:16 says: 'Confess your sins to each other and pray for each other so that you may be healed.'

And 5:14 instructs us to go to elders for the anointing of oil.

Many Christians believe they'll be healed by getting zapped at a meeting, or by reciting some verses. But the bible doesn't guarantee that. People might get a temporary reprieve, but the healings often don't last.

God's healing is personal

God also said in Exodus 15:26 that he is our personal physician. 'I AM the Lord who heals you,' he proclaimed.

He doesn't offer one-size-fits-all healings. His cures are made-to-measure.

The word 'heal' in Hebrew means to *stitch together, to cure, darn, mend, repair, to pacify.* These are tasks that are done personally and carefully.

Jesus said that God numbers each hair on our heads. And he also knows your DNA, and every part of your body, soul and spirit.

Psalm 139:14 says we are fearfully and wonderfully made. And with God as our physician, we can be fearfully and wonderfully healed.

Father is not a healing force, or a method, where you dig around in your past and tick things off a list, or endlessly recite bible verses.

You can teach a parrot to say: 'By his stripes I am healed.' But it'll remain as sick as a parrot, and so will you if you ignore God's covenant conditions.

So much healing leaves Jesus out. We give people earthquakes, wind and fire at conferences and meetings. But we ignore the still small voice of our personal physician, the I AM.

Religious rubbish

People say some strange things when they're not healed.

They proclaim: 'God's teaching me something.' But they must be slow learners, as they have often been ill for years. And when you ask them **what** he's teaching them, they often don't know.

Or they say: 'This sickness is the cross I have to bear.' But the cross was where God **removed** sickness. Jesus bore it, so we don't have to.

Some say with solemn faces: 'Brother, I'm sharing in Christ's sufferings.' But did Christ suffer illness? No.

Or they may say: 'This illness is my thorn.' But God only allowed Paul's thorn because he had incredible visions and revelations. If you have a thorn without similar revelations, you're kidding yourself.

And in any case, there is no evidence that Paul's thorn was a sickness.

Then there are those who say: 'This sickness is God's will.'

This makes me wonder why they take medicine and go to the doctor. If God wants them sick, they shouldn't try to recover.

God's Treatment Plan

I once visited a friend in hospital after he suffered head injuries in a football match.

I'm nosey, so I browsed through the Personal Treatment Plan hanging at the end of his bed.

It said he needed his ankle re-set and an MRI scan on his back, which I thought was an unusual way of treating concussion.

In fact, they'd swapped his plan with someone else's.

Father God has a Personal Treatment Plan for you, and he won't mix it up with anyone else's.

He knows exactly why you are ill, and how to get you better again.

Jesus used Personal Treatment Plans, too.

He healed one blind man by spitting on the ground, making mud and rubbing it in his eyes. Then he told him to wash it off.

But he healed two other blind men by touching their eyes.

And another time, he took a blind man out the village and spat on his eyes and laid hands on him twice.

In Jewish culture, spitting at someone was utterly insulting. It made them ceremonially unclean. So, in effect Jesus told him: 'Hey mate, now you're unclean as well as blind.'

Why? Because this man was unique. He needed a Personal Treatment Plan from the physician's Son.

These days, one of those blind men would have written a book called: 'Three steps to healing using spit and mud.'

Another might have started the Church of the Holy Saliva. Dribble preached every Sunday.

You also see divine Personal Treatment Plans when people were raised from the dead.

Elijah laid on top of a dead body three times before God revived it. But Elisha only did it once.

Perhaps Elijah needed three goes because he lacked faith!

Jesus waited four days before he called his dead friend Lazarus out the tomb.

But he just touched the widow of Nain's son's body and Jairus' daughter and told them to get up.

Later, Peter knelt by a dead girl and prayed, and she was raised back to life, whereas Paul achieved the same result by taking a dead man into his arms.

Each miracle was different because each person was different.

Jesus used Personal Treatment Plans for people's recoveries, too.

He told the demoniac to go back to his family, the man at the pool to stop sinning, and instructed lepers to show themselves to the priest.

So, if you're sick, ask Father God for your Personal Treatment Plan. But be warned, you will have to follow it.

It might involve a miracle now, or later. Or it might be a process. It might even mean a stay in hospital.

You can't do it on your own terms.

Namaan, the commander of the king's army tried that in the Old Testament (2 Kings 5:1-19).

He wanted God to heal him from leprosy, so Elijah told him to bathe seven times in the River Jordan. This was like telling him to repeatedly jump into a sewer.

But Namaan was Very Important and wanted Elijah to come to him and call on the name of the Lord. Religious and respectable.

But Elijah wouldn't compromise, Namaan capitulated, and was healed.

In the same way, God may ask us to change our beliefs, alter our lifestyles, forgive people, or deal with wrong attitudes and sin before he heals us.

But his Personal Treatment Plans are perfect and practical. And there's one for everyone in the church that Jesus builds.

Jesus also told us to heal other people.

There's never been a better time for churches to preach the word with signs following (Mark 16:17-18).

Thousands of people have Long COVID. Others are sick and dying because the NHS is failing. It will get worse.

Healing for non-Christians is easier. They are not bound by the covenant, and Jesus often heals them to reveal his love. That's what he did for me.

Three types of healing

Sometimes, when I pray for someone to be healed, nothing seems to happen.

But in fact, God is usually answering prayer, just as he promised.

The New Testament reveals three types of healing. And God knows which is best for each person.

First, there are miracles.

All four gospels use the same Greek word for the word 'healed'. It means *'instantaneous, miraculous'*.

Most of Jesus' healings were instant. And we want them because they're spectacular.

But only God knows whether people can cope with the emotional, mental and social changes that a miracle involves.

30

The blind beggar whom Jesus healed (Luke 18:35-43) probably had to get a job. The woman who touched his robe had to rebuild relationships after years of exclusion and shame. The demoniac went back to his family.

Miracles have consequences. I know a disabled woman who was healed overnight. She left her wheelchair at home and went to church.

But, she lost her benefits, her carer's allowance and had to relearn many household skills.

Some people would prefer to remain disabled.

Second, there are **gradual recoveries.**

Jesus said: 'They shall lay hands on the sick and they will recover.' And the Greek word for *recover* is *kalos* and means *'full well'* or *'whole'*. It's a **process** that involves physical healing and wholeness in soul, spirit, family, finances and all the things that make up each person's complex ecosystem.

Third, healing can be **part of your salvation.**

Salvation means more than going to heaven when you die. When Peter said in 1 Peter 2:24: 'By his wounds we are healed,' he used the word *sozo,* or *'to save'*.

But *sozo* also means to *deliver, protect, heal, preserve and make whole.*

God wants to restore people's spirits and souls, not just for now, but for eternity. Physical healing is just part of the package.

Word and Spirit

I help to lead Freedom Church, and we have seen God perform more than 150 miracles over the past two years. Most of them involved people who had lost hope.

We pray, he does the rest.

God has healed most of the COVID-19 victims we have prayed for since April 2020. Many were dangerously ill in hospital and not expected to live.

One man, a church pastor near Cape Town, South Africa recovered so quickly that he started prayer services in his hospital ward.

We have also seen housebound and bedbound people healed and able to go out.

And there have been several cases where suspected cancer tumours disappeared before surgery.

One lady who burnt her hand was instantly healed and didn't even have any burn marks. And another woman was healed of hernia after 28 years and later had the sight in her blind eye restored.

One couple conceived a child after being childless for 20 years and God also quickly healed new-born baby who fighting for her life in ITU.

A lady's doctor was puzzled because she no longer needed a heart operation, and another woman with weight problems lost two stone in five weeks.

One woman no longer uses her wheelchair and can go out for walks.

These miracles have bewildered us. But we are learning that when we allow the Word of God and the Spirit of God to work together, signs will follow the word.

That's how it should be in the church that Jesus built.

The church that Jesus builds will routinely experience miraculous healings and recoveries.

Chapter 3

BLESSED ARE THE RULE BREAKERS

I recently looked at some job adverts for church administrators. They mentioned qualities like admin/IT skills and a good telephone manner.

But none mentioned the spiritual gift of administration (1 Corinthians 12:28). This struck me as odd.

Perhaps the applicants had this gift. But the advertisers apparently didn't see it as a priority.

An administrator who lacks the spiritual gift of administration may build worldly systems that conflict with the way Jesus builds his church.

Without the Holy Spirit, administration will lead to legalism, rigidity, hurt and control.

I once met an African pastor who laughed when I said that my church had an office. He couldn't work out why.

His church 'just' had a prayer room. It grew from 60 to 600 in two years. And he still didn't have an office.

'Jesus will see you now' ...

When Jesus met two of his first disciples, he didn't tell them to book an appointment or say: 'We must have a coffee some time.'

He took them home (John 1:35-39). After that, he continued to minister in homes as well as public places.

The same happened after Pentecost, too (Acts 2:46-47).

Buildings and procedures often prevent Jesus building his church, because they focus on ... buildings and procedures! Not people.

And in a society dominated by IT and controlled by legal policies, we must fight to stop churches becoming organisations. Yours may be one already.

The church that Jesus built was organised, but it wasn't an organisation.

Jeremiah 2:13 warns that God's people who build their own cisterns will be cursed. That's why so many manufactured churches have closed.

They started in a blaze and collapsed in a daze of bureaucracy.

Why? When they grew, they used secular systems to keep control. And remember, Satan is the prince of this world.

That doesn't mean the church that Jesus built was disorganised. Far from it. It had a treasurer, a support team and planned wisely.

When Jesus sent the 12 disciples on their first mission trip, he told them where to go, what to do and what to take.

Later, he arranged a room for the Last Supper and a donkey for his ride into Jerusalem.

He planned missions in advance and arrived in Jerusalem for important festivals. This involved more than booking a donkey on Uber a few hours a before he left.

Jesus used the gift of administration to streamline his mission. And he always put people before procedures.

He broke religious and cultural rules, not to be rebellious, or for personal gain, but because people were more important.

He must have been great fun to work with.

Mission or 'Mishnah'?

The Pharisees called their book of man-made traditions the 'Mishnah'. Most churches have their equivalents, and people are routinely damaged by them.

Some are denied prayer because of the 'Mishnah'. The bible tells us to lay hands on the sick. But some churches add rules that prevent it.

I was once sternly rebuked for praying for a man in urgent need, because I didn't get his house group leader's permission first.

So, the bible says: 'Lay hands on the sick.' But the 'Mishnah' said: 'Get consent first.' The result? The guy didn't get prayer and left the church.

I visited another church where a man I knew asked me to pray for him. He was distressed and needed help. But as I prayed, I noticed the pastor standing nearby, hands on hips, shaking their head in disapproval.

God touched the man powerfully. But the pastor couldn't celebrate because I broke the 'Mishnah'. They had rules about who was allowed to pray for who.

The incident reminded me of the Pharisees' reaction when Jesus healed the man born blind. The rules were more important than the miracle.

It's called legalism. God hates it, and we all must guard against it.

We all have an inner Pharisee who wants to impose rules. But Godly administration should help to **meet** people's needs more effectively, not deny them.

Religion often walks past on the other side. In the parable of the Good Samaritan, the Priest and the Levite decided that their religious duties were more important than helping a dying man.

In contrast, the Samaritan adapted his schedule and risked his reputation and possibly his life by helping a Jew. In those days, the hatred between the Jews and Samaritans was as great as it is now between Hamas and the Jews.

The Good Samaritan wasn't the first to discover that showing love in a legalistic environment is dangerous. It's the same in some churches.

A flexible friend

Jesus used supernatural administration to great effect in Matthew 14.

When he heard that his cousin, John the Baptist had been beheaded, he wanted to spend time on his own. So, he sailed off to a remote area.

But 5,000 people turned up, needing help.

He could have stuck to his schedule and sent them way. But he adapted, amid his grief.

He taught them and fed them, again using administrative skills to organise them and clear up afterwards.

Then, he sent his disciples off in a boat, and eventually found time to be on his own.

After that, it gets exciting. He was late. So, he walked on water to catch up them up.

So, he didn't scrap his schedule or lose sight of his goal. He miraculously adapted it to meet people's needs. That's supernatural administration.

If we put people first, the Holy Spirit will plug the gaps. But the religious people will wave the 'Mishnah' in anger.

Aye aye, captain

The Greek word for the spiritual gift of administration is *kubernesis*. It refers to a ship's captain, who steers a boat towards its destination.

So, church leaders say: 'Here's where we're going.' And the administrator says: 'I'll get you there.'

But sailing in New Testament days depended on the wind. So, a true administrator should follow the wind of the Spirit and find ways to get you to God's destination.

In contrast, a worldly administrator will probably tell you why you **can't** get there ...

There's not enough money. It's against government policy. It's a designated gift. The trustees won't like it. It breaches safety regulations or the data protection laws. We need a risk assessment. Sound familiar?

Official or not?

I helped to lead a church in the poorest part of East London, and the pastor wouldn't have known a procedure if he saw one.

But he understood how Jesus built his church.

He told me many times: 'Look for the life.' So, when he saw the life of the Spirit flowing, he joined in. But if an activity looked lifeless, he allowed it to die.

If a group of people enjoyed meeting together, they became a house group. What else could they be? After all, they were a group that met in a house.

And if some folks met to pray … well, that was a church prayer meeting. Again, what else could it be? Jesus said that if two or three people turned up, he would be there too. How much more approval do you need?

One meeting emerged at 10pm on a Saturday night and attracted more people than the 'official church prayer meeting' on a Tuesday evening. Awkward.

Many pastors would have closed the 'unofficial' one. But what biblical right does a leader have to stop people praying? So, he kept both, and as a result, more people got involved in prayer.

We just watched God move and joined in.

Many leaders won't allow gatherings in homes in case they 'go wrong', cause trouble, or become a breakaway group. But where's the faith in that? They are paralysed with fear, and slaves to the 'Mishnah'.

Faith comes by fearing …?

Frightened leaders love rulebooks. Rules eliminate risk. But they also eliminate faith.

Leadership means taking risks and trusting Jesus with the outcome.

It's messy, but if you want a quiet, uneventful environment with nice, tidy rows, then visit the cemetery. Or a 'manufactured church'. There's little difference.

Jesus once sent his 12 relatively unprepared disciples on a mission trip. We'd ask them to sign a health and safety disclaimer first.

The great Pharisee Gamaliel knew how God worked. When confronted with a new, noisy church in Jerusalem, he said in Acts 5:39: 'If their purpose or activity is of human origin, it will fail.

'But if it is from God, you will not be able to stop these men; you will only find yourselves fighting against God.'

Sadly, many leaders prefer to fight God than ditch the 'Mishnah'.

Risk assessments are now routine parts of church life and they can make biblical Christianity impossible.

I wonder what Jesus' risk assessment for the feeding of 5,000 looked like. Eating fish in the hot weather. No hand washing facilities. No toilets. No food. Not quite the Big Church Day Out!

Yet they saw blessings, not bands and miracles, not music.

Spirited leadership

The book of Acts reveals that the 12 apostles did not often plan any significant initiatives in the Jerusalem church. They usually reacted to circumstances, to needs or to the Holy Spirit.

They wouldn't recognise our churches, with our procedures, rotas and action plans. And they might ask why we use them when they don't advance the gospel like their Spirit-charged methods did.

Jesus told us to take no thought for tomorrow, and yet most church administrators can tell you what's happening for the next 12 months - times, dates, venues, speakers, the lot.

Or maybe they **can't** tell you because data protection law stops them.

Self-built churches that use secular procedures, rules and structures usually quench the life of the Spirit. They also hurt or even expel people who don't conform.

They label rule breakers as rebels.

But if you put a rule ahead of a person in need or create a structure around something that God hasn't initiated, Jesus is not building your church.

And if you love those enticing secular systems and procedures ... well, you may get the prince of the world as your boss.

The church that Jesus built was founded on faith.

Without that, it is impossible to please God.

I no longer call you servants ... I call you data subjects

Over the past 20-30 years, many churches have become organisations, not organisms.

They have swapped the Messiah for methods, faith for formulas and power for procedures.

This is extraordinary, because Jesus said in John 3:8: 'The wind blows where it wishes and you hear the sound of it, but do not know where it comes from and where it is going; so is everyone who is born of the Spirit.'

How can you possibly create a method out of that? And why would you want to? Only if you're after money, power or control, or lack the faith that Jesus **can** build his church.

He did incredible miracles, signs and wonders because he had the Holy Spirit without limit.

And yet we think this isn't enough and add our own methods and marketing.

Why? Because methods are easy. They don't require faith.

Why wait on the Lord when you can open a book? Why walk on water when you can stay in a boat with an instruction manual?

Miracles happen when the unvarnished word of God and the unrestrained Spirit of God work together.

Church life should be risky and unpredictable.

He IS, you ISN'T

Methods, 'Mishnahs' and manuals miss one vital truth.

In Exodus 3:14, God told a startled Moses: 'I AM WHO I AM. This is what you are to say to the Israelites: "I AM has sent me to you."'

I AM is the ultimate description of God - if one is possible.

It shows him as the God who will be what he will be, who is eternally constant, ever-present, self-sufficient and unchangeable. A God who does what he wants to do.

And the implication of I AM is: 'YOU'RE NOT.'

If we use a manual instead of the Messiah, we say to God: 'I am. You're not. I'll do this my way.'

And this takes us back to two places.

Place One: nude food

First, we revert to the Garden of Eden, where the serpent presented Eve wisdom (Genesis 3:1-7) from the tree of knowledge. She decided that it looked good. It always does.

But it left her and Adam sinful and naked. It does that, too.

James 3:15 talks about two types of wisdom. One comes from God. The other is earthly, unspiritual and demonic. That's what the serpent offered.

One is light, the other darkness.

The Hebrew word for Satan's wisdom means *rational, circumspect, prudent. To consider carefully, comprehend … to think carefully before saying or doing anything.*

Do those words describe your church? Probably. We live in a rational world. And look at the mess.

These 'qualities' seem so utterly reasonable but are the **opposite** of God's wisdom.

When Moses sent 12 spies to the Promised Land, ten of them reported back, using worldly wisdom.

They said in Numbers 13:27ff: 'It really is a land flowing with milk and honey. Here's some of its fruit.

'But the people who live there are strong, and the cities have walls and are very large.

'We can't attack those people! They're too strong for us!'

How rational and carefully considered. Prudent. A sensible risk assessment. Stay at home. Save lives. Protect the status quo.

But then Caleb spoke God's wisdom. First, he told people to shut up and listen to Moses. That's a good place to start - listen to the man or woman of faith, not the person with the rule book.

Then he said: 'Let's go now and take possession of the land. We should be more than able to conquer it.'

He saw the same things as the other 10 spies but used Godly wisdom, which brings faith.

Judas used worldly wisdom when Mary poured nard on Jesus' feet during dinner with Lazarus in Bethany (John 12:1-7).

He asked why the perfume wasn't sold and the money given to the poor. After all, it cost a year's wages.

Very prudent. So rational. Any church treasurer would be delighted. And Gift Aid it too.

But Jesus then presented God's wisdom. He said: 'You will always have the poor among you, but you will not always have me.'

His reply wasn't rational or fair. But it wasn't supposed to be.

Place 2: tower power

Manufactured methods also take us back to the Tower of Babel. Men said in Genesis 11:4: 'Come, let us build ourselves a city, with a tower that reaches to the heavens, so that we may **make a name for ourselves**.'

That Babylonian build-it-yourself spirit is still an enemy of God's church.

It is in ascendancy now.

Many Christians try to 'ascend to heaven' through their own efforts and human achievement. It's based on ambition.

They try to make names for themselves on their church websites and build a following on social media.

But there's no faith involved. Romans 10:17 says: 'Faith **comes** by hearing God's word.'

That word *comes* in Greek means *'to emerge from the inside'*, like giving birth, whereas books, manuals, websites and human reasoning come from external sources.

They appeal to our souls. And to the 'Mishnah'. And the church's policy-powered administrator.

Psalm 127:1 says: 'Unless the LORD builds the house, those who build it labour in vain.'

This verse cuts through our methods, structures and procedures. Our job is to labour. But God builds. He is I AM.

We're not.

By titles, everyone will know you are my disciples ...

Jesus told his disciples in Matthew 23:8 that his followers shouldn't use titles.

He said: 'You are not to be called 'Rabbi,' for you have one Teacher, and you are all brothers.'

Clear enough. If your church is a true family, you won't need to a title to show how important you are. And the statement 'you are all brothers' removes the concept of hierarchy.

And yet we have a Christian landscape overcrowded with Reverends, Fathers, Bishops, and even the occasional Executive Leader.

How people square this with Jesus' commands is beyond me.

In the same way, Paul only referred to himself as Paul. Or Paul, an apostle, never The Apostle Paul. And certainly not St Paul.

Peter did the same. Not Pope Peter. And the five-fold ministries in Ephesians 4:11 were roles, not titles.

But I've yet to find a church that doesn't use titles. Why?

Being a Reverend doesn't make you reverent and calling yourself a leader doesn't mean people follow you.

Christian service is about who we are, not what we call ourselves. This is why Paul said in 2 Corinthians 10:12: 'We do not dare to classify ourselves.'

In Colossians 4:7, Paul referred to a guy named Tychicus as a beloved brother, faithful minister and fellow servant.

These terms mean far more than some fancy title.

The day that churches abandon titles will be the day when we can say that Jesus is truly building them.

The church that Jesus builds will not resemble a secular organisation.

Chapter 4

DO TWO WALK TOGETHER? NOT ALWAYS

In January 2019, more than 3,000 Christians and a team of respected leaders assembled in London for a National Day of Prayer.

It was a wonderful display of unity.

But, soon afterwards, some groups published statements on their websites, disassociating themselves from things they saw and heard.

They mentioned 'the enemy', 'error' and 'unbiblical practices and beliefs' and provided a public platform for other Christians to spew their ungodly attitudes and insults.

Many did just that. They by hurled abuse, made unsubstantiated slurs and passed on gossip.

This took place in the year before COVID-19. Maybe if there had been greater unity, things might have been different. But answered prayer requires agreement (Matthew 18:19).

This debacle was nothing new. Renowned preachers use YouTube to name fellow believers and brand them agents of the devil. But scripture condemns this behaviour.

2 Timothy 2:16 says: 'Avoid godless chatter, because those who indulge in it will become more and more ungodly.'

And Galatians 5:19 says that enmity, strife, jealousy, rivalries, dissensions, divisions, and envy are sins of the flesh. It mentions them in the same breath as drunkenness and orgies.

Paul said in Ephesian 5:11 that deeds of darkness are fruitless. So, if an individual or organisation bears God's fruit, it is not a deed of darkness.

It might do things differently and get things wrong. But so has every church since the one Jesus built with his disciples. And that's OK.

God has been sorting out his people's mistakes since the Garden of Eden and he's good at it.

Sticks and stones break God's heart

It's OK to disagree with other Christians, like Paul did with and Barnabas and Peter. But we must never call other believers names, or use labels like false prophets, backsliders, lukewarm, or uncommitted. Our tongues have the power of life and death (Proverbs 18:21).

Name-calling is nothing new. Jesus was called Beelzebub, demonised, insane, a glutton, a drunkard, a friend of sinners, a blasphemer ...

Most of those insults came from religious people. It's the same now.

In contrast, the 'common people' called Jesus a prophet, Master, the Christ or the Messiah.

Name-calling merely exposes our rudeness, our religious attitudes, our self-righteousness and the darkness in our own hearts.

Believer or deceiver?

It's become fashionable to say that Christians with whom we disagree are 'in deception'.

It's a grave accusation, as it brackets them with Satan (Revelation 12:9 and Matthew 24:24).

The bible is clear how to handle allegations like this. The accuser must produce two or three witnesses to establish the truth (Deuteronomy 19:15, Matthew 18:16, 1 Corinthians 13:1).

If they can't do that, they are just gossips, or 'tale bearers' if they repeat their claims.

We might disagree with other Christians. But that doesn't mean they are deceived or are deceiving others.

Paul had a huge disagreement with Peter. He said he was wrong (Galatian 2:11-13) - and he was. It took Peter around 15 years to fully understand that the Christian faith included Gentiles. However, Paul never said Peter was deceived.

And yet some believers throw the word 'deceived' around like sweets at a kid's birthday party, and with the same level of maturity.

The bible says we should test everything (1 Thessalonians 5:21), but not **everyone.** We should weigh prophecy (1 Corinthians 14:29), but not those who prophesy, other than look at their fruit (Matthew 7:16).

It's not our job to separate the wheat from the tares. God's angels will do that at the end of the age (Matthew 13:24-43).

If you think other believers are wrong, you should speak to them personally and keep it between the two of you (Matthew 18:15-17), not scream at them from a webpage.

If you do, Matthew 7:2 says: 'In the same way you judge others, you will be judged, and with the measure you use, it will be measured to you.'

One body, many parts

Now, the church that Jesus built never split.

Eleven of the original 12 disciples stayed together until the Jerusalem church was scattered by persecution.

When Peter stood up at Pentecost to address the crowd, the other 11 stood up with him (Acts 2:14). And they weren't gathering information to use against him!

So, how did they achieve this? How did they become a church that was 'one in heart and mind' (Acts 4:32)?

Paul says it was the fruit of the 'mighty power that is at work within us' (Ephesians 3:20). In other words, it was humanly impossible.

Acts 4:32 gives us another clue. They were **believers.**

True believers will not dare to accuse others or speak against them.

That's why most name-calling in church life comes from people with religious attitudes. They don't behave like believers. You show me a name-caller and I'll show you a Pharisee.

The Pharisees who confronted Jesus in John 8:39ff **thought** they were believers. They were confident that they had one Father: 'God himself.'

But Jesus put them straight: 'You are from your father the devil.'

You cannot achieve unity by attending business meetings, agreeing 'core values' or signing a mission statement.

Unity is a heart attitude that comes from having a revelation of Jesus. And when you truly love him, you would never consider dividing his body or publicly insulting other Christians, even when they are wrong or deserve it.

Love to agree, agree to love

There has been a lack of biblical understanding about unity which has ironically created division.

Unity is often construed as agreeing with the leaders or supporting your church's 'vision'. And if you disagree, you may be shown the door, labelled a rebel or even expelled.

This is why having a 'vision' is divisive. It forces people to decide if they're behind it. But it's not a choice they need to make.

In contrast, having a vision of Jesus, the head of the church, brings unity.

Leaders must fear God. They're dealing with his flock, not their own personal fiefdoms.

Some leaders use Titus 3:10 to kick people out 'their' church. This verse says: 'Warn a divisive person once, and then warn them a second time. After that, have nothing to do with them.'

But the previous verse says this step is for people who are involved in **divisive false teaching**. No-one else.

Leaders who have disciplined people for being divisive just because they held a different opinion should apologise to them.

And if they disciplined them publicly, they should apologise publicly.

The unholy trio

Three things cause division.

First, ignorance of scripture.

The New Testament refers to unity of the Spirit **and** unity of the faith.

Unity of the Spirit doesn't mean joining a denomination, supporting the church's mission statement, or agreeing with an apostle's revelation.

Paul says in Romans 6:5 that we **have** unity of the Spirit if we believe in Jesus and are born again of the Holy Spirit.

After that, we must make every effort to preserve it by living a life of the love described in 1 Corinthians 13:4-6.

It never fails.

Unity of the **faith** means agreeing with the core truths taught by Jesus and the apostles in the bible, not manufactured add-ons.

And we must be realistic. Paul says in Ephesians 4:11-13 that we need the five-fold ministry to achieve unity and maturity.

You may feel horrified when you hear the word 'apostle'. I don't blame you. Men and women have turned this beautiful calling into a repulsive and godless system of money, power and control.

But Paul says in 2 Corinthians 12:12 that true apostles will demonstrate signs, wonders and miracles. And they don't charge.

Using these criteria, I've only met two apostles in 45 years as a Christian - a couple called Norman and Grace Barnes.

Second, tribal thinking.

Most of us draw a circle around our group, our family, church or denomination, and exclude or even attack everyone outside it.

This is what the disciple John was like. In Luke 9:49, he told Jesus: 'Lord, we saw someone driving out demons in your name and we tried to stop him, **because he is not one of us.**'

'Do not stop him,' Jesus said, 'for whoever is not against you is for you.'

Have you got a 'not one of us' mentality like John? I have. But Jesus said there's no 'us and them' if we're for **him.**

The new covenant abolished the 12 tribes. We are a priesthood, united in love and belief by Jesus.

Third, hardness of heart

Jesus once said that divorce was permissible because people had hard hearts (Matthew 19:8).

And division in the body of Christ is like divorce, as it severs spiritual relationships.

Hard hearts make us judge people who do things differently. We see their faults and not our own. We believe we're right and that God is on our side. As if!

Joshua had this mentality. Joshua 5:13ff says: 'Now when Joshua was near Jericho, he looked up and saw a man standing in front of him with a drawn sword in his hand. Joshua went up to him and asked, "Are you for us or for our enemies?"

"Neither," he replied.

'Then the angel added: "Take off your sandals, for the place where you are standing is holy.'"

Next time you think God is on your side in a dispute, remember - you're standing on holy ground.

Holy ground invites you take the plank out of your own eye, humble yourself and meet those you disagree with, not gossip about them or shout at them from emails and social media.

And remember, Father God is most unlikely to be on your side, even if, like Joshua, you are in the right.

He cares more about love and unity than who's right and who's wrong.

Most church splits are caused by hard hearts. People are prepared to damage other believers, families and even whole communities to get their own way. They lie, curse and accuse each other.

They don't realise they are wounding God. Or if they do, they don't care.

Avoiding a split decision

Genesis 13:5-13 shows how to handle a possible split.

Abraham and Lot's shepherds were quarrelling over land. So, there's nothing new!

But peace and unity were more important to Abraham. So, he didn't fight for his rights as landowner and family patriarch, even though he could have done.

Instead, he let Lot choose the best land.

And he acted with courtesy. The Hebrew language in Genesis 13:8ff suggests he was clear, firm and polite when they discussed the problem.

Abraham also had generous heart. Earlier, he offered his son Isaac to God as a sacrifice. So, after that, he may not have found it difficult offering Lot the best deal.

And he knew that God would keep his promises in the long-term, so how could he lose?

Then later, he even risked his life to save Lot when he was in trouble.

That's how to avoid a church split.

If someone in your congregation wants to plant a church, then let them choose the best people and the location. Release them with your blessing and support.

And if they get into trouble, rescue them, even if it costs you your life.

Then, God will honour you and keep his promises.

But if you harm his son's body, he will oppose you. He will probably place a lid on your ministry, and won't remove it until you repair relationships, apologise and make restitution.

People who divide the body of Christ sow the wind, and usually reap the whirlwind (Hosea 8:7).

The fab four

There are four things we can do to achieve unity of the faith.

First, ask the Holy Spirit to truly reveal Jesus to you. When he does, divisive manufactured techniques won't seem so important, and we will start behaving like believers rather than religious r

Second, repent of John's 'not one of us' mentality and watch out for it in future.

Third, promise God that you will never publicly malign another believer or Christian organisation. Remember, true believers will never behave this way.

Fourth, pray for a biblical five-fold ministry in your church.

If we all stick to these, our churches will be living examples of 1 Corinthians 13:4ff: 'Love is patient, love is kind. It does not envy, it does not boast, it is not proud.

'It does not dishonour others, it is not self-seeking, it is not easily angered, it keeps no record of wrongs.

'Love does not delight in evil but rejoices with the truth.

'It always protects, always trusts, always hopes, always perseveres.'

The church that Jesus builds will always give preference to other believers.

Chapter 5

STEAL FROM THE POOR, GIVE TO THE RICH

I've had some odd things happen to me in church.

One woman was sick over me. Not great before a two-hour drive.

Another lady punched her pastor in the face when I prophesied: 'God really loves you.'

His wife said later that she wished she'd done the same. I was glad the pastor was standing next to this lady and not me!

Then, another time I was charged to attend a church prayer meeting.

No kidding. Although Jesus had paid the price to give me free access to God's throne, I still had to pay at the door.

I imagined the disciples asking Jesus: 'Lord, teach us to pray' (Luke 11:1), and Jesus replying: 'First, go to the cashpoint …'

And what about people who paid on instalments? Would their prayers be answered on a Pray-as-you-go basis?

This incident revealed how secular churches have become.

I knew a lovely guy who had a big van that God gave him. He used it to bless people by giving them lifts and delivering this-and-that. That was his ministry until the Lord took him home in 2020.

He never charged for his petrol, or his time. To me, he was a spiritual giant.

I knew another guy who had a song that God gave him. He used it to bless people. That was his ministry.

But in contrast, he sold his song to a Christian recording company and became very rich.

What's the difference? If God gives us something, do we have the right to make money from it? Jesus never did.

Freely receive, freely charge

The bible mentions two people who charged for their gifts.

One was Balaam, who was hired to use his supernatural power to curse Israel.

The other was a slave girl whom Paul confronted in Acts 16. She made money from divination.

We might shake our heads in disgust, but then charge people to go on a prophecy course. There's no difference.

Jesus opposed people who cashed in on their faith. He expelled the money changers and traders from the temple courts. Ministry is not a business.

Micah 3:11 condemns prophets who told fortunes for money. Micah also shrewdly observed that they prophesy that everything will be fine ... 'No disaster will come upon us.' Paid prophets still say the same today, because 'nice' words grow audiences.

1 John 1 says we should be enemies of the world, so how can we bring secular thinking into God's gifts? Yet most big-name ministries I have encountered over the years have done very well out of it.

If God is in something, he'll pay for it. And if he doesn't, question it.

Finance made easy

New Testament teaching on money was terrifyingly simple.

John the Baptist wasn't joking in Luke 3:11 when he said we should give away a coat if we have two. My first pastor lived like that.

Jesus started his ministry by calling some fishermen away from their jobs. This was a big statement about priorities.

His team depended on other people's hospitality as they travelled from town to town. They didn't have a reliable supply of food or shelter.

That's why the disciples ate grain from someone else's fields (Matthew 12:1). This was a custom reserved for the poor.

And although Jesus had a home, he didn't always have somewhere to 'rest his head' (Luke 9:58). No five-star hotel and payment up front for him when he was on the road.

He was supported financially by a lady named Susanna and some other women.

But Jesus even used some of that money to feed the poor. And when all else failed, he trusted God for a miracle, like finding a coin in a fish to pay the temple tax (Matthew 17:27).

Jesus never asked people for money or dropped hints about his needs.

I have some friends who have been missionaries for around 40 years. But they never mention money. Their prayer letters are exactly that, not thinly disguised fundraisers.

None of us should use God's promises to improve our lifestyles.

We have a duty to live as cheaply as possible and give the rest to the poor.

We can't say we're good stewards if we live more expensively than we need to while people die of starvation.

Silver and gold, we have plenty

I once visited a church in a very wealthy area, and I reckon the congregation's combined assets were around £1billion. And yet the box for the food bank contained two packets of porridge and a tin of beans. Shocking.

James 2 says our faith is dead if we don't help people in need. The longer I am a Christian, the more I realise how dead my faith really is.

We have swapped influence for affluence, signs for sign-ups, beggars for buildings, power for projectors and charismata for concerts.

People in the church in Jerusalem shared everything they owned so everyone had enough.

They sold property and gave the money to the apostles, who passed it to those who needed it (Acts 4:35). They **didn't** use it to fund their own lifestyles.

Rich young rulers, and older ones too

Now, I am strongly in favour of tithing and giving.

But many churches misuse tithes and rob the poor. And God is calling for change.

In the Old Testament, tithes went to the high priest (Genesis 14:20), the priests, the Levites (Numbers 18:21), or the temple (Nehemiah 12:24).

But, under the new covenant, **Jesus** is the temple (John 2:19-21) and the high priest (Hebrews 4:14). And according to 1 Peter 2:29 you are as much a priest as your local vicar.

So, perhaps you should consider bringing your tithes to Jesus, and asking him what to do with them.

If he invites you to give to your local church, that's great.

But we cannot ignore Deuteronomy 26:12: 'When you have finished setting aside a tenth of all your produce in the third year, the year of the tithe, you shall give it to the Levite, the foreigner, the fatherless and the widow, so that they may eat in your towns and be satisfied.'

In both the Old and the New Testaments, tithes and gifts were used for the poor, for refugees, for the fatherless and for mission.

There's no mention of giving a slice to an apostle, your denomination or to pay the church secretary.

Churches have a sacred duty to spend people's tithes and offerings in the fear of God.

Scripture does not say that they can be used to pay salaries, or to cover leaders' travel expenses.

Father has strong words to leaders who do this. Ezekiel 34:3 says: 'You eat the curds, clothe yourselves with the wool and slaughter the choice animals, but you do not take care of the flock.'

The Hebrew word *care* means to provide for them, not just pop round for a cuppa and a prayer.

When Nehemiah became governor of Jerusalem, he refused government funds to pay for his family's meals, even though he was fully entitled to them.

He paid his own way. That's the standard we should follow.

Any pastor or leader who uses people's tithes to fund their lifestyles should consider publicly apologising and making restitution. If God has called them to their ministry, he will pay for it.

God cannot be mocked

I knew a devoted old lady who saved £5 from her meagre pension for an itinerant evangelism team, who lived by faith. It was a huge sacrifice, as she lived just above the breadline.

I was there when she proudly and tearfully gave the team leader her fiver.

Moments later, I heard him say to a friend: 'Beer money for our next gig.'

And that's where it went. I felt God's anger burn. The team soon folded up with their dreams and prophecies unfulfilled.

I heard of another church that used people's tithes to pay for a Christmas dinner for its leadership team and their partners.

I wasn't surprised to hear, two years later, that the church was in financial trouble.

You can't take God for a fool.

Are you cursed?

People often ask me to pray for them, as they believe they may have been cursed.

The fact is many of us have been. Proverbs 28:27 says: 'He who gives to the poor will never want, but he who shuts his eyes will have many curses.'

If you feel you're under many curses, that might be why.

Jesus said we should give to anyone who asks. We won't enjoy full salvation unless we do.

Isaiah 58:11 says: 'The Lord will guide you continually, and satisfy you with all good things, and keep you healthy too; and you will be like a well-watered garden, like an ever-flowing spring.'

What a promise. But it's **conditional** on feeding the hungry and helping those in trouble. You don't hear many prosperity teachers quote this verse in full.

Our stinginess can beggar belief

I went to a church where the vicar spoke about love. He said the King James Version used the word charity to emphasise that love means **doing**.

Now, a beggar was standing outside the church, asking people for money as they left the service.

But most of them walked straight past him, without a gift or even a Hello. Oh, the irony.

I recalled James 2:16ff: 'If a brother or sister is poorly clothed and lacking in daily food, and one of you says to them, "Go in peace, be warmed and filled," without giving them the things needed for the body, what good is that?'

Now I'm sure everyone could justify why they didn't give anything to that beggar.

'He'll spend it on drink.'

'He's there every week. He should find a job.'

'He knows Christians are a soft touch.'

'Charities say that giving to beggars makes them worse.'

I've used all these excuses and maybe you have, too.

But Jesus made giving simple. He said: 'Give to those who ask.' (Matthew 5:42).

Maybe this guy was taking advantage. So would I, in his situation. But he was poorer than me and the well-heeled people in the meeting.

So, we had a duty to give. No excuses. As the vicar said, *agape* love means **doing.**

Do you pass the love test?

John's first epistle is one of the most challenging books in the bible.

He says in chapter 3:17: 'If anyone has material possessions and sees a brother or sister in need but has no pity on them, how can the love of God be in that person?'

How much of God's do I have in my heart? According to this verse, not a lot.

Christians could bring tens of thousands of people out of poverty if we wanted to.

We shouldn't rely on the government, social services, a charity or a food bank to do it. It's our responsibility to help.

Hired hands get their P45s

God has used the COVID-19 pandemic to remove thousands of salaried pastors, leaders and other hangers-on from church payrolls.

Why? Because many are robbing the poor of their tithes. But there's another reason.

When Jesus restored Peter on the shores of Lake Galilee, he pressed him on one key issue: 'Do you love me?' (John 21:15ff).

Peter eventually said 'Yes,' and **then** Jesus replied: 'Feed my sheep.'

Jesus doesn't want people feeding his sheep unless they love him. Otherwise, they may do it for status, power or money. Or all three.

Jesus called payroll pastors 'hired hands' in John 10:12. He said they abandoned the sheep when they were attacked.

So, God used COVID-19 to separate them from true shepherds.

True shepherds will look after their sheep, even if they get other jobs. But career Christians will abandon them because their love depended on payment.

Churches that are facing post-COVID-19 financial hardship may have to publicly repent of their corrupt stewardship, and then make restitution by giving their money to the refugees, the fatherless, the poor and the widows.

Then, perhaps their gospel will be worth hearing.

The church that Jesus builds will never retain money for itself.

Chapter 6

DON'T BURY YOUR TALENT (OR ELSE!)

I t's bewildering why people who want to follow God's call, often have to go outside their local church.

If they want to praise and worship freely, they attend a Filling Station or similar.

And if they want to use the gifts of the Spirit, they join a clandestine group and hope nobody finds out.

So, the local church then ends up as a religious social club, while God's cutting-edge stuff takes place somewhere else. This makes me wonder which is the church that Jesus is building!

I believe Father is deeply saddened because many churches are structured to prevent new ministries emerging.

Denominations have constitutions, hierarchies and rule books.

And newer churches that were founded on body ministry are now like High Anglicans, with a 'clergy' on the platform and a laity - or audience - that watches.

This is far removed from the church in Corinth, where everyone wanted to take part (1 Corinthians 14:26). 'Spectator' is not a church ministry.

Jesus sent his 12 disciples to cast out demons and to heal every disease within around 12 months of calling them (Matthew 10:5).

And then he sent out 72 to do the same later (Luke 10:1). Six groups of 12. Think about that. It's called church growth.

Churches should be places where people are fast-tracked to follow God's call.

God is looking for clay pots to contain his power, not polished vases from a bible college or an expensive training course.

He uses imperfect people who are humanly ill-prepared. And this goes against the secular thinking that has permeated so many churches.

Sorry, but you can't preach the gospel ...

Many churches are ministry bottlenecks.

I prayed for a man who was disillusioned and depressed. He had a passion for local evangelism, but his leaders said it didn't fit in with their 'vision'.

So, here was a church that was opposed to saving souls. Hmm.

I asked him: 'What other vision can there be?' I advised him to obey the Great Commission (Matthew 28:16ff) and 'Go' even though his leaders said: 'Stay.'

Old men (and women) will do nothing ...

Older people are often side-lined by churches who gladly take their index-linked tithes, but who mirror the UK's adulation of youth.

Many seniors become spiritual spectators when they turn 70, even though they have the wisdom that comes from walking with God for decades.

Some have led successful churches, headed up mission teams, and had fruitful, God-approved and powerful ministries.

But they end up stacking chairs and making coffee in churches that have flipped scripture, so that older people are led by the young.

Isaiah 3:4 says young leaders are a sign of God's judgement.

Of course, God will raise up young Timothies, Samuels and Jeremiahs. Some commentators reckon that some of Jesus' disciples were teenagers. I pray there will be thousands more of them.

But biblically, mature believers should mentor them. And elders should be - old!

Mighty mentors

Jacob mentored his youngest son Joseph effectively.

God started speaking to Joseph in dreams when he was 17. And like most young beginners, he was headstrong and arrogant. He boasted to his brothers, and it nearly cost him his life.

Eventually, he told his father what had been happening. He should have done that in the first place. Fathers guard visions. Brothers often steal them.

Jacob rebuked Joseph, but 'kept the dreams in mind' (Genesis 37:11). Perfect mentoring.

Yes, the teenager needed to sort out his attitudes. But Jacob didn't reject Joseph's revelations. He had encountered God himself and recognised that the Lord might be speaking to his son.

Scripture mentions other mentors, too. Jethro trained Moses, Elijah trained Elisha, and Paul trained Timothy.

The bible says that older people should bear fruit in old age (Psalm 92:14).

That means doing miracles like Moses, waging war like Caleb, interceding like Anna, seeing like Simeon, bringing new birth like Abraham, prophesying like Jacob, and writing letters like Paul and John.

Churches are the losers if they don't.

I have heard many prophecies about God 'raising up a generation of young people', but none about God mobilising a generation of side-lined old ones.

Churches pay lip service to people like Caleb, but then fill their leadership teams with under 30s who have gifting and passion but lack wisdom and the experience that comes from walking with God and knowing his ways.

So, most over-70s 'finish the race' by cooking microwave meals rather than conquering mountains like Caleb did.

Some are side-lined by technology. I once asked a lady why she had stopped welcoming people at the church door.

She tearfully told me that the church administrator decided to post the rotas online. She didn't know how to use the internet.

What a tragedy. And I wondered, who was more important, the person or the process?

Use your gift: that's an order!

So, if you are side-lined, it's your responsibility to ask God to release your ministry.

The parable of the talents says we **must** use the talents that God has given us. Jesus declared that people who didn't were worthless, and would be cast into outer darkness, a place where there was weeping and gnashing of teeth.

This sounds like hell, though I'm not making a theology out of that! But 1 Corinthians 3:13 does say that God will test quality of each person's work by fire.

I am not sure he will be too convinced if you say: 'Oh, my leader wouldn't let me do anything.'

1 Peter 4:10-11 says: 'Each of you should use whatever gift you have received to serve others, as faithful stewards of God's grace in its various forms.'

Each of you means just that. No ifs or buts.

And Paul reminds us in Ephesians 2:10: 'For we are God's handiwork, created in Christ Jesus to do good works, which God prepared in advance for us to do.'

God didn't just create you. He created your mission, too. You were born with it, and it's a leader's job to help you fulfil it.

God frequently released ministries in the bible, without men or women being involved.

In Exodus 31:3, he bypassed Moses and appointed Bezalel to build the tabernacle. And he filled him with the Holy Spirit, too.

He only told Moses about it afterwards.

It's ironic that the name *Bezalel* means '*in the shadow [protection] of God*'. People whom God raises up often need divine protection!

The Lord also raised up Joseph, Elijah, Paul, John the Baptist, Gideon, Jeremiah, Isaiah and many others.

And when he wanted a successor to Elijah, he bypassed the bible college students - the school of prophets - and chose a farmer.

The biographies of people like Jackie Pullinger, Smith Wigglesworth, Kathryn Kuhlman and William Booth show that they heard God's call and got in with it, sometimes alone. Their churches caught up later. Sometimes, they didn't.

Go and bear fruit (but get permission first)

Many Christians believe that they can only function if their leaders say so.

Of course, some ministries and roles must be recognised and appointed by the church leaders or the congregation.

But leaders do not have the authority to stop someone following God's call.

Their role is to serve, advise, disciple people, and oversee the moral, doctrinal or relational aspects of their churches.

They cannot prevent people from saving souls, doing prayer walks, praying for the sick, casting out demons, caring for others or becoming missionaries.

Or from hosting their own bible studies, prayer meetings, or worship evenings.

But many try. They stop people ministering because they are afraid. But that's control: the sin of witchcraft.

Jesus said in John 15:16: 'I chose you and appointed you so that you might go and bear fruit.'

What else do you need to know?

Please release me ...

In 2017, I was frustrated about fulfilling my calling. Years were ticking by, and I knew God had more for me to do.

Then one day I heard him say: 'How long are you going to wait for men to release your ministry?'

So, I asked him to release me. And he did - in his own way.

I was ill and depressed for the next six months. Father cut me to the chase. I ended up so weak, I couldn't function.

Then he said: 'Go in the strength you have' (Judges 6:14). And later he added: 'Do what's in your hand.'

So, I started a blog and making podcasts. It's not what I expected, but I had to prove to Father that I could be trusted with small things.

Then, two years later, he told me to start a work that became Freedom Church in 2020.

Knock knock

If God releases you, it doesn't mean doing your own thing or using him as a rubber stamp for some pet project or idea.

Your job is to knock. And then God will open the door (Matthew 7:7) when he's ready. If you break the door down, cause disunity or promote yourself, you'll get nowhere.

God sometimes puts a 'lid' on people if they force their way into their ministry. He restricts whatever they do.

Others try DIY ministry and usually produce an 'Ishmael'.

An 'Ishmael' is the product of our flesh … something that is conceived out of impatience and produced by human reasoning rather than by faith.

We're all capable of producing one. In fact, it's easier to produce an 'Ishmael' than to wait for God's promise. Abraham discovered that when he conceived a child with Hagar (Genesis 16:2).

And once you've created an Ishmael, you're stuck with it.

It will cause you frustration and heartache and will never produce spiritual fruit. It can't, for things that are conceived in the 'flesh' remain flesh. And products of the flesh are in permanent conflict with the Spirit (Galatians 4:29).

So, asking God to release you is **not** the easy option.

He will oppose you if you harm Jesus' precious body or dishonour his anointed leaders.

And he won't release you if you are bitter, proud or rebellious, or have an 'I'll show 'em' attitude.

God's boot camp

If you ask God to release you, he will also put you on his programme to train you to be a son or daughter. And that involves discipline and pain.

Jesus spent 40 days without food in the wilderness. Do you fancy that?

Moses spent 40 years there.

Joseph spent time in a pit and a prison before he worked in the palace. How does that sound?

God will relentlessly examine your heart and confront your motives and your attitudes.

Only Jesus can provide authority, favour and legitimacy. If you carry heaven's approval, people will recognise your credentials. If you don't, then you'll labour in vain.

If you cooperate, God will make space for you like he did with Isaac in Genesis 26:22.

It says: 'Isaac dug another well, and no-one quarrelled over it. He named it Rehoboth, saying, "Now the LORD has given us room and we will flourish in the land."'

And if he raises you up, you won't have to discover your ministry. You won't be able to contain it.

You won't have to tell people what you do. They'll tell you. You won't need a title or a badge. People will recognise you.

You are anointed already

Few Christians know what the anointing is! It's one of the most misused words in the Christian vocabulary.

You hear people say: 'There was a strong anointing on that meeting.' Or: 'That song was really anointed.'

But most of this is twaddle.

Anointing with oil emerged in the Old Testament. Shepherds poured oil on each sheep's head to prevent lice and other insects getting into its ears and killing it.

Then, over a period, people began to be anointed with oil to symbolise blessing, protection and empowerment by the Holy Spirit.

And now, you are anointed when you become a Christian.

Paul says in 2 Corinthians 1:21: 'Now it is God who makes both us and you stand firm in Christ.

'He anointed us, set his seal of ownership on us, and put his Spirit in our hearts as a deposit, guaranteeing what is to come.'

Remember, Paul was an apostle, and when he said **you and us**, he meant he was no different to the Corinthians.

Now, Corinth was a moral cesspit, where sexual immorality was accepted as normal.

And the church was the same. One bible scholar says the Corinthian church was involved in 'gross, unashamed immorality'.

And yet Paul still said they were as anointed as he was.

Why ask for what you've got already?

People often stampede to 'get the anointing' at meetings, but 1 John 2:20 says: 'But you **have** an anointing from the Holy One.'

John wrote this epistle to people in several different places. He didn't know them all personally or where they stood with their faith.

But he still said: 'You have an anointing.'

For him, if they were believers, that was enough.

So, you are already anointed with the Holy Spirit to empower you in your ministry.

The anointing isn't just for doing signs and wonders for super saints, who speak at big conferences.

You are as anointed as they are, whether you visit the sick or raise the dead.

Only God can anoint you

The anointing and the baptism of the Spirit are two different things.

In the New Testament, the men and women laid hands on other people, to baptise them in the Holy Spirit (Acts 8:1-25).

They imparted gifts of the Spirit to them (1 Timothy 4:14). And they set them apart for mission and ministry (Acts 13:2-3).

But only God anointed them (2 Corinthians 1:21b).

Please release me

There's a difference between having an anointing and using it.

And you can only use your anointing when God releases it. There are no short cuts.

In the Old Testament people were anointed with olive oil, which was obtained by beating ripe olives.

Exodus 27:20-21 says: 'Command the Israelites to bring you clear oil of beaten olives for the light so that the lamps may be kept burning.'

That word beaten in the Hebrew means to *break into pieces.*

So, after God has anointed you, he allows you to be beaten by many difficult situations, to release the purest oil of the Holy Spirit. This produces light and your lamp will burn powerfully.

No quick fix

Many people do not fully use God's anointing because it hurts. So, they look for shortcuts.

They try to grab someone else's power or position, start a DIY ministry, or get some big name to lay hands on them.

It's a waste of time. You can't force God's hand.

So, maybe reflect on the beatings you've had from family, church, sickness and circumstances. God was using them to release your anointing.

If this doesn't seem fair, look at it this way.

The bad stuff happens anyway, and either makes us **better** or **bitter.** It's our choice.

The difference between these two words is **I**. And **I** usually stands in the way of anointing and effectiveness. **I** must die!

When we become Christians, we give Jesus the right to do what he likes with us.

His salvation is a life of blessings and beatings, power and pain, victories and vitriol.

We get the bad bits anyway. So, we might as well allow God to extract miraculous good from them.

Anointed to wait

David the shepherd boy was anointed as king when he was quite young. And what did he do? He went back to his sheep and served King Saul (1 Samuel 16:19-22).

God doesn't usually release his anointing in a hurry. First, he watches to see if we can look after sheep, and whether we are willing to serve someone else.

After that, David suffered an attempt on his life by his father-in-law, a plot to kill him involving his best friend, and deep grief.

He was pursued by his enemies and hid in caves and deserts.

Then he became king.

And even then, the beating didn't stop.

He had to fight many battles and face his personal failings when he committed adultery.

Later, his daughter was raped. Then he was usurped by Absalom and had to fight to get his crown back. Then he had to deal with another rebellion.

But his anointing exalted the one true God, and produced stunning victories. It created a strong system of government across Israel. It established Jerusalem as a religious centre.

David also wrote Psalms that have helped hundreds of desperate people over many centuries. And he is now known as a man after God's own heart (1 Samuel 13:14) who served his generation well (Acts 13:36).

God will use life's beatings to extract pure oil of anointing from you. It will produce remarkable results.

Planning your prison break

So, what do you do if your church does not create space for you?

First, speak to your leaders. And listen carefully if they say no. They may have valid observations, and you would be foolish to ignore them.

After that, ask Father God to release you. But remember, God rarely calls people to minister alone.

Jesus sent two people to collect a donkey for the triumphal entry, and two to book a room for the Last Supper. Only Judas ministered alone (John 12:6).

Even the Lone Ranger had Tonto!

Then, deal with the fear of other people. Paul said in Galatians 1:10: 'If pleasing people were my goal, I would not be Christ's servant.'

Many people never become Christ's servants because they want to please others.

Then check your life. Is it blameless? Psalm 84:11 says: 'No good thing does God withhold from those whose way of life is blameless.'

Being blameless is a forgotten key to fruitful ministry.

Then, get hungry. Call out to God to make room for your gift, your ministry.

Ask and keep on asking. Seek and keep on seeking. Knock and keep on knocking until he responds.

He will.

It will be risky, painful and messy at times. And that's the good bit!

The church that Jesus built will ensure that imperfect people are empowered to do the work that they were born for.

Chapter 7

GIVE NICE A CHANCE

E ven non-believers know that Christianity is about 'being nice'.

But many Christians don't get that. We tend to be heavy-handed with our pastoring and discipling.

This is wrong. The word 'gentle' is used more than 20 times in the epistles, because the church that Jesus builds is founded on gentleness.

Hebrews 5:2 describes the qualities of an Old Testament High Priest.

It says: 'He is able to deal **gently** with those who are ignorant and are going astray, since he himself is subject to weakness. This is why he has to offer sacrifices for his own sins, as well as for the sins of the people.'

So, we must be gentle with people when they mess up, because we're no better than they are. Sadly though, hierarchical leadership structures often produce leaders who think they have an elevated status.

They control who can speak to them or pray for them. Their stance when sorting out a problem with someone is: 'I'm right, you're wrong.'

I once attended a church leadership training session on 'How to confront people.'

I was horrified. That word confront has no place in church relationships. It is the opposite of gentleness.

The bible only mentions it in the context of confronting an enemy, or God confronting us.

Fellow believers are brothers and sisters, not enemies. Our job is to win them, restore them and maybe correct them.

Paul says in Galatians 6:1 says: 'If anyone is caught in any transgression, you who are spiritual should restore him in a Spirit of **gentleness**.'

Clearly, gentleness is a sign of spirituality.

Paul adds in 1 Thessalonians 2:7: 'We were gentle among you, like a nursing mother taking care of her own children.'

You don't get much gentler than that.

Philippians 4:5 says: 'Let your gentleness be evident to all.'

Is your gentleness evident to your brothers and sisters in church?

To a gay guy? A racist? A teenager struggling with their gender? To a sex offender? A refugee? A political opponent?

Our society is starting to require us to be selective in our love and gentleness, the same as in pre-war Nazi Germany.

But **all** means **all**.

How not to do it

Paul told his young apprentice Timothy (2 Timothy 2:24) to correct opponents **gently** and not to rebuke an older man harshly (1 Timothy 5:1).

I once witnessed a young leader who had only been saved four years reduce a man in his late 70s to tears as she 'confronted' him. It was one of the most disgraceful episodes I've seen in church life. It was unkind and unbiblical.

The man was a gentle, mature servant who had faithfully served God for decades. In contrast, the leader was still in God's nursery and acted like it.

Another time, a young leader with three years salvation behind her met a mature woman of God in her 70s to 'shape her up' (her words).

More arrogance. More tears.

In both cases, I couldn't fathom how these 'baby Christians' could possibly think that they had anything of value to say to seasoned, mature believers. They should have been asking for their help.

Peter was a strong, hot-headed character. But he said (1 Peter 5:3) that leaders should not be domineering and set an example.

People with domineering characters shouldn't be leaders. But they often end up in positions of authority because of ambition and the force of their personalities.

None of us should correct anyone until we learn gentleness. Some of us never do.

The Greek word for 'domineering' is *katakyrieuontes* and means to *subdue someone, to overcome them, or overpower them.*

It is derived from the same word as 'to condemn', which is Satan's job. Enough said.

Paul shows a better way in Romans 15:1-2. He says: 'We who are strong ought to bear with the failings of the weak.'

The Greek word for *to bear* is *bastazein*, which means to support or carry. And *failings* is *asthenēmata*, which means weak, sick or impotent.

This is God's instruction to all Christians, especially those who enjoy confronting someone who doesn't live up to their expectations.

They quote Proverbs 27:1: 'As iron sharpens iron, so a man sharpens the countenance (face) of his friend.'

But the word 'sharpen' comes from the Hebrew root that means *fierce and severe sharpness.*

And in the Old Testament, *sharp facial features* are only mentioned when someone intended violence or destruction.

So, the phrase 'iron shaping iron' was never intended to mean something positive.

Church leaders who use words like 'confront', should mind their language. And their behaviour.

The New Testament shows a better way.

Jesus sometimes spoke sternly to people, but as a servant who was prepared to wash his disciples' feet (John 13:1-17).

Leaders are called to be servants and slaves (1 Corinthians 9:19), and to lead by example (1 Corinthians 11:1 and Philippians 4:9).

If they need to correct someone, they should take the planks out their own eyes first.

And they should be prepared to be wrong rather than 'put the other person straight'.

Biblically, they should only bring correction to church relationships, morality and doctrine. They have no right to micromanage your life ... who you can see, which meetings you should attend.

And none of us may impose our own standards, culture or expectations on other people. We are called to make disciples of Jesus, not ourselves.

Many fine men and women have lost their way and even their faith after being dominated by leaders with strong characters or manipulated by those with weak ones.

Such leaders often quote Hebrews 13:17, which says: 'Obey them that have the rule over you.'

But they don't study the scriptures. The Greek word for *obey* comes from two root words ... one means *persuade*, and the other means *faith*.

If a leader needs to correct someone, they should persuade them in a way that produces faith, not fear, pressure or condemnation.

In situations like this, the New Testament uses the words *admonish, reprove and rebuke*. But English makes them sound harsher than the bible.

In the Greek, *admonishing* means *reasoning* with someone by *warning* them. The root word, *nouthe* means *training by word*, and does not often mean *chastise*, as it does in English.

Paul only uses this word twice, in his letter to the Colossians 1:28, and Colossians 3:16.

Similarly, *reproving* means *convincing someone with solid, compelling evidence.*

And *rebuking* means *warning someone by instructing them.* Paul urged Timothy to do this with 'complete patience and careful instruction'.

The only time he recommended a 'sharp' rebuke was when Titus faced a group of rebellious people who were making money out of false teaching (Titus 1:10-16).

I've seen people rebuked sharply for a lot less than that in church life.

In addition, leaders should never pressure people or overwork them.

Jesus condemned the Pharisees for doing this in Matthew 23:4: 'For they bind heavy burdens, hard to bear, and lay them on men's shoulders; but they themselves will not move them with one of their fingers.'

Jesus came to set people free from the yoke of slavery.

Leaders should make sure they keep it that way.

Here is the forecast

We live in a harsh and merciless world, where people are exposed to the Twitter mob, 'cancelled' without hope of restoration or pronounced guilty before they are tried.

Paul prophesied this in 2 Timothy 3:2-5. He forecast a society that was abusive, without love, unforgiving, slanderous, brutal and lack self-control.

In contrast, the church should be a place of mercy and love, where people are forgiven, restored and given as many second chances as they need when they fail or do wrong.

Harshness is now enshrined in many UK laws. And churches that have adopted them will eventually have to decide whether to follow God's ways of love and mercy, or society's cruel diktats.

Many churches use cruel secular 'procedures'. They treat allegations as fact, and don't allow people a second chance.

The church that Jesus builds carries a message of hope and restoration to every human being.

Chapter 8

BORN FREE

I was once asked to pray for a family at the end of a meeting. The husband and wife and their three children were all sobbing uncontrollably, clinging to each other for comfort.

They were traumatised, crushed and afraid. I wondered if they'd been involved in an accident or tragedy.

In fact, they had endured three years of cruelty by leaders of a Christian house church.

Their wills had been violated, their characters assassinated, their relationships undermined, their ministries destroyed.

Then they had been labelled as rebels and kicked out. All because they 'didn't do as they were told'.

They weren't alone. I've prayed with many other people who have been crushed, mistreated and excluded by churches.

Soon after I was saved, a close friend was offered a new job. He was thrilled but turned it down because the pastor told him to.

I was appalled.

Controlling leadership is, of course, nothing new.

But if a leader overrides your will, demands obedience, manipulates you, dominates you or intimidates you, then it's witchcraft.

Witchcraft is a sin of the flesh. You don't have to join a coven to practice it. And it's contrary to Jesus' teaching. He came to set captives free (Luke 4:18) and said that the greatest among us must become everyone's servant (Matthew 23:11).

Then he showed what he meant by washing his disciples' feet and then being tortured and killed because he loved them so much.

Take back control

Churches have a long history of mistreating and controlling people.

During the 1970s, five prominent American Christian leaders known as the Fort Lauderdale Five introduced 'discipleship' teaching that badly damaged thousands of Christians across the world.

They taught that Christians should submit to human authority and account to men and woman rather than to God.

And people were pressured to swear covenant relationships with friends, pastors and churches, which could only be broken on the pain of judgement. Terrifying.

The 'shepherding' movement was responsible for hundreds of cases of spiritual abuse. Some, like the family I prayed for, never recovered.

And this discredited teaching is still promoted in many evangelical and charismatic churches, even though most of the original proponents have publicly acknowledged it was wrong.

The Fort Lauderdale Five eventually split up. At least two of them of publicly apologised.

One said: 'We were guilty of the Galatian error: having begun in the Spirit, we quickly regenerated into the flesh.'

Fine-sounding religious language. I prefer to rephrase it: 'We were guilty of introducing witchcraft, bullying and control that damaged large numbers of people.'

I have prayed with many people who were deeply affected. Some lost their ministries, their marriages, even their faith. Others were traumatised and had breakdowns.

A bit more serious than a 'Galatian error'.

Claim your gift

Personal freedom is God's gift and possibly the highest expression of his love. It was fundamental to the church that Jesus built.

Before creation, the angels were free to submit to God, or not. One third didn't.

Adam and Eve were free to obey God or not. They didn't.

In the Old Testament, the Jewish race was free to follow God. Sometimes, they did, sometimes they didn't.

They were even free to kill God's son Jesus. They did.

Jesus was free to choose what to do when the devil tempted him in the wilderness and when he struggled in Gethsemane.

He brought a gospel of freedom and unconditional love, so we are no longer slaves to him or anyone else.

But it's easier to coerce people than to serve them, and easier to boss people around than to die for them.

Free indeed

I'm not saying church should be a free-for-all. Just that there must be **freedom for all**.

Freedom to attend meetings or not. Freedom to worship. Freedom to disagree, to challenge, to make mistakes, to have a different calling or do things differently.

Jesus never controlled anyone because control is the opposite of love.

He never checked if the woman caught in adultery followed his advice (John 8:11).

He didn't pressure the rich young ruler to make a decision (Mark 10:22).

He allowed his disciples to accept or reject his teaching. In fact, in John 16:67, he asked them: 'Do you want to leave, too?' No pressure. No demands.

He didn't demand allegiance from the disciples at the Last Supper or expect their loyalty when he was arrested.

He gave Judas the freedom to betray him, and Peter the freedom to disown him. Both did.

Love sets people free.

In contrast, the Fort Lauderdale Five's teaching was based on three main components: covering, accountability, and covenant relationships.

Covering uncovered

I was chatting to someone recently, and he asked me: 'Who's covering you?'

I said: 'God.'

He looked at me as if I'd said: 'The devil.'

My friend believed that the God who is my healer, provider, protector, deliverer and so many other things couldn't cover me as well as a human could.

How ridiculous. And what a narrow, faithless view of Father.

Covered by a fig leaf

The 'shepherding' movement taught that a leader had God's authority to 'cover' a person's decisions and protect them from deception and sin.

But only God can cover his people.

No-one has the right to say what another believer can or can't do.

Legitimate leaders should have hearts like Gideon, who told the men of Israel in Judges 8:22-23: 'I will not rule over you, neither shall my son rule over you: the Lord shall rule over you.'

Covering by humans is nothing new.

When Adam and Eve sinned (Genesis 3:7) they covered themselves with fig leaves.

But these weren't adequate, so God covered them with garments that he made from animal skins.

Covering is his job, not ours. And it involves shedding of blood. In contrast, covering by men and women is as effective as a fig leaf.

Isaiah 61:10 says: 'For God has clothed me with the garments of salvation, he has **covered** me with the robe of righteousness.'

Covering is also part of his covenant of love.

Ezekiel 16:8 says: 'I passed by, and when I looked at you and saw that you were old enough for love, I spread the corner of my garment over you and covered your naked body.

'I gave you my solemn oath and entered into a covenant with you,' declares the Sovereign Lord, 'and you became mine.'

Which human being would dare to stand in the place of God, or try to hijack his covenant with his people?

Do it God's way

The Old Testament uses two Hebrew words for 'covering'.

The first is *sukuk,* which means *to protect, cover, defend, or hedge in.*

God himself was Israel's protector. Psalm 91:1 says: 'He who dwells in the secret place of the Most High shall abide under the shadow of the Almighty.'

The Hebrew word for *'secret place'* means to *cover, provide a hiding place, or protect.* So, if we dwell under Almighty God's covering, we are safe.

The Psalm adds that the Lord rescues us, covers us with his feathers, and shelters us under his wing.

Which human being can offer protection like that?

In Psalm 28:7, David describes how God kept him safe, hid him in the shelter of his sacred tent and set him high upon a rock.

He was writing from experience. He had faced Goliath, fought countless battles, lived in fear of his life and faced plots and schemes. But God covered him.

Psalm 146:3 makes an important point: 'Do not trust in princes, in mortal man, in whom there is no salvation.'

We should never trust rulers for, or with our salvation. Psalm 3:8 says salvation comes from the Lord. Then we work it out with fear and trembling (Philippians 2:12).

The second Hebrew word for covering is *cafa,* which means *to make atonement.*

It is used in Leviticus 16, when Aaron slaughtered a goat to cover the people's sin.

But under the new covenant, only Jesus can cover our sins by shedding his innocent blood on the cross (Romans 3:25).

Being covered by men or women is futile. And it diminishes God's unlimited ability to care for you.

No accounting for accountability

You often hear calls for the government or politicians to be 'held accountable'.

You also hear it in many churches. But it has no place there.

One glossary defines it as: 'The obligation of an individual to account for their activities, accept responsibility for them, and to disclose the results in a transparent manner.'

God never obliges us to do anything. He lets us decide.

The bible does not use the word 'accountability' in relation to church government or discipleship.

It only appears in the New Testament when Jesus said people were accountable to **God** (Matthew 12:36).

In the Old Testament, the word appears in Daniel, when referring to the tyrannical Babylonian regime.

Daniel 6:1-2 says: 'It pleased King Darius to appoint 120 satraps to rule throughout the kingdom, with three administrators over them, one of whom was Daniel.

'The satraps were **made accountable** to them so that the king might not suffer loss.'

The Babylonian empire was governed by a hierarchical system, with brutal accountability at every level. If you got something wrong, you could pay for it with your life.

The Hebrew word *'accountable'* in Daniel 6:2 is *ṭaʿ·māah*, and refers to a top-down military command structure.

Now, in the bible, Babylon represents secularism. Its values are the opposite of God's. In fact, Revelation 17:5 refers to Babylon as 'the mother of prostitutes'.

So, why would we use the mother of prostitute's values in church government, discipleship, or anything else?

Any church that operates a hierarchical system of leadership misses the heart of Christian life.

Jesus' hierarchy puts the leaders at the bottom, as 'the servants of all' (Mark 9:35).

In Matthew 20:25-28 he said: 'You know that the rulers of the Gentiles lord it over them, and their high officials exercise authority over them.

'**Not so with you**'. Instead, whoever wants to become great among you must be your servant, and whoever wants to be first must be your slave - just as the Son of Man did not come to be served, but to serve, and to give his life as a ransom for many.'

Note the words: '**Not so with you.**' He couldn't have made it clearer.

He added in Luke 22:25-27: 'Who is more important, the one who sits at the table or the one who serves? The one who sits at the table, of course. **But not here!** For I am among you as one who serves.'

Again, note the words: '**But not here.**'

For who is greater?

I once went to a leaders' conference saw an 'apostle' snap his fingers at someone and say: 'Get me more coffee.' And I remember thinking: 'Actually pal, if you're the boss, you should be getting the coffee.'

After all, Jesus said in Luke 22:7: 'I am among you as one who serves.'

Many people are more accountable to their leaders than they are to God. This makes the leader a mediator and enters dangerous territory.

1 Timothy 2:5 says: 'For there is one God and one mediator between God and mankind, the man Christ Jesus.'

Accountability in church life often comes with obligation, coercion, heavy-handedness.

It frequently lacks grace, mercy, redemption and forgiveness. And it creates fear of losing your ministry, your position, or of being side-lined or rejected if you don't make the mark.

This produces people-pleasing and gives leaders power that God does not intend them to have.

Checking in? Check it out

Perhaps we should replace 'accountability' with **'checking in'**. Who do you check in with? Far gentler. And more biblical.

Jesus created a loving environment where his disciples happily checked in with him.

In Luke 9, he sent the 12 on their first mission, and then 72 later.

They checked in with him when they returned. Not because they had to, or because he needed to grill them about everything they'd done.

The bible says they reported back with excitement and joy (Luke 10:17).

Jesus never demanded accountability from his disciples in the church that he built.

He gave people the freedom to make their own choices.

He gave Judas the freedom to steal, cover it up, and then to betray him.

He also gave Peter the freedom to quit, and then the freedom to either follow his calling or remain a fisherman.

He gave the rich young ruler the freedom to walk away.

This is true love.

Now I'm not advocating independence.

1 John 1:7 invites us to walk in God's light. So, we **should** share our lives, our sins, our strengths and our weaknesses with people we trust.

But we must also gently bear with each other's weaknesses, show mercy, and cover other people's sins with love.

I have two or three trusted friends with whom I share everything.

They pray for me and support me with love, prayer and correction.

I would encourage you to do the same. Tell someone everything, especially the worst stuff. It's not easy, but it brings true freedom.

This is especially important for leaders. Any leader who isn't completely transparent with someone as well as their partner is open to deception … and so is their congregation.

How you check in

Now, checking in must be done biblically.

You must ask for it. No-one can require it from you.

Everyone involved must take the plank out of their own eyes (Luke 6:42) and submit to one another (Ephesians 5:21).

And they should respect people's confidences, and never share anything with anyone else.

I once confided in a pastor, who told me he needed to tell his wife so he could be transparent with her.

I politely pointed out that he was required to be transparent about his life, not mine!

Covenant relationships? Welcome to the coven

During the 1980s and 1990s, friends and even entire churches swore solemn oaths before God to remain together.

And more seriously, many invited judgement on themselves if they broke the covenant.

People cursed themselves. And the results were catastrophic.

Covenant relationships are unscriptural and potentially dangerous.

I've heard - and am still hearing - terrible stories of divorce, rape, calamity, family break-ups, premature death and terminal illness among people as a result of these self-imposed curses.

Words are powerful. They really do have the power of life and death (Proverbs 18:21).

You're bound to agree

The first five letters of the word *covenant* spell COVEN, which is a gathering of witches. The word has its root in French and means 'to agree'.

People who join witches' covens, Satanist groups and other cults usually swear an oath of loyalty - a *coven*ant - and bind themselves to the people they agree with.

They also invite punishment on themselves if they break the terms.

Covenant relationships lead to exclusivity and control and have no part in the church that Jesus built.

Many churches who promoted covenant relationships had reputations for being cults. Some of them were.

Their love depended on your agreement. If you kept the covenant, and you were fine; but if you broke it, you were excluded, the same as the Jehovah's Witnesses, who disfellowship people who leave. Serious stuff.

No strings attached

Jesus' love is unconditional. He never crosses people's wills or pressures them into obedience.

He did not ask for allegiance from his disciples, and only introduced them to one covenant - the one he signed in his own blood.

Christians may only enter two covenant relationships.

One is with God, and the other is with their husband or wife. Both covenants are biblical and bring a blessing.

Other covenant relationships are wrong because people end up with two covenant masters - Jesus Christ, and a person, or a group of people.

And Jesus said no-one can obey two masters. You cannot fulfil a covenant with a man or a church without compromising Jesus' lordship over your life.

No swearing, please

Jesus told his followers not to swear oaths. In Matthew 5:34, he said: 'You have also heard that our ancestors were told, "Do not make any vows! Just say a simple, 'Yes, I will,' or 'No, I won't.' Anything beyond this is from the **evil one.**"'

And James 5:12 reinforces the point: 'Above all, my brothers, do not swear, not by heaven or earth or by any other oath. Simply let your "Yes" be yes, and your "No" be no, so that you will not fall under judgement.'

These verses are clear: vows and oaths are of the devil. This gives him the right to enforce them instead. And he does.

Normally, a Christian is protected from curses, because God promises in Proverbs 26:2 that an undeserved curse does not come to rest.

But people who invoke judgements and curses on themselves deserve them because they asked for them.

And their words will 'rest on them' and may wreak havoc until they are renounced and broken.

Get out - quick

Proverbs 6:4-5 instructs anyone who has made a pledge or a vow to get out of it urgently.

It says: 'My son, if you have put up security for your neighbour, if you have shaken hands in pledge for a stranger, you have been trapped by what you said, ensnared by the words of your mouth.

'So do this, my son, to free yourself since you have fallen into your neighbour's hands: Go - to the point of exhaustion - and give your neighbour no rest! Allow no sleep to your eyes, no slumber to your eyelids.

'Free yourself, like a gazelle from the hand of the hunter, like a bird from the snare of the fowler.'

Ungodly spoken agreements will ensnare us and must be ended. The passage also says they are difficult to break and how powerful they are.

You are not bound to your church

We should never swear allegiance to a church, a denomination or a vision.

Some leaders ask people to swear an allegiance to themselves. But this is godless and dangerous, as it places you under their control.

The early Christians faced death if they didn't swear allegiance to the man-god Caesar. They would only swear allegiance to God.

Yes, you should give your leaders honour and your elders double honour. But never pledge allegiance to anyone or anything other than Jesus.

Church membership isn't biblical either, so make sure you read the terms and conditions before you sign up.

The shepherding movement brought in dangerous false teaching that is still around today.

Don't be fooled. Jesus came to set you free. Make sure you keep it that way.

The church that Jesus builds will prioritise the freedom of the individual.

Chapter 9

IT'S TIME TO MOVE OUT

When the Jewish people wandered in the wilderness for 40 years, God set strict rules on cleanliness and sanitation.

His social distancing guidelines involved designating an area **outside the camp** (Deuteronomy 23:12).

It was a refuge for people who were sick, infected, who suffered skin diseases and leprosy, or who were 'unclean' for various reasons (Leviticus 24:14, Numbers 5:2-4).

Ash and animal carcasses were dumped there, too (Exodus 29:14, Leviticus 4:21). And people were executed there (Numbers 15:36, Leviticus 24:14).

But it was in this filthy, disgusting area that our holy God took up residence.

Exodus 33:7ff says: 'Moses used to take the tent and pitch **it outside the camp,** a good distance from the camp, and he called it the tent of meeting.

'And everyone who sought the Lord would go out to the tent of meeting which was **outside the camp.'**

We would have pitched it in a nice field and served latte at the entrance.

Or we'd book a hall with a band, lights and a sound system. Or meet in an historic building, with purified priests and sanitised choristers.

But our holy God met his people outside the camp.

And verse 9 adds: 'Whenever Moses entered the tent, the pillar of cloud would descend and stand at the entrance of the tent; and the Lord would speak with Moses.'

So, the glorious presence of God was **outside** the camp.

Jesus' presence in the garbage tip

Jesus spent a lot of his time outside the camp, too.

He met an unclean woman by a well and offered her salvation to drink (John 4:13-14).

In Mark 1:40, he healed a disgusting leper by touching him, and then swapped places with him. The man remained in the town while Jesus left it.

Jesus also touched corpses (Mark 5:41), spoke to unclean Gentiles and trod on cursed ground to bring freedom to a maniac (Luke 8:26-39).

Each time he went outside the camp, he became unclean under Mosaic law.

Finally, he was executed outside the camp. Golgotha was outside the city walls - home to Jerusalem's unfit, unclean, and unwanted.

What's that got to do with the church that Jesus builds? Everything.

Fast forward to Hebrews 13:12: 'Jesus suffered **outside the city gate** to make the people holy through his own blood.

'Let **us,** then go to him **outside** the camp, bearing the disgrace he bore.'

Oh.

During the COVID-19 lockdowns, we were told to save lives by staying indoors.

But now, we must go **outdoors**. Outside the camp, and share Jesus' disgrace, rather than getting counselling for it.

It will mean leaving the safety, comfort and religious formalism of 'Jerusalem' to meet Jesus in that filthy, disgusting place.

It means rejecting the commercialised, organised, systematised and risk-free perversion of Christianity and swapping conferences for compassion, festivals for filth, and tea at church for the fleas of the unchurched.

Clearing the temple courts

Many of us have been spoon-fed inside the camp, with a cosy, me-first religious philosophy.

But this 'temple courts' faith funds affluent apostles, makes profits for prophets, and turns pastors into hired hands.

No wonder God brought it to a shuddering halt with the COVID-19 pandemic.

'Inside the camp' Christianity encourages us to focus on ourselves. **Our** needs, **our** feelings, **our** victory, **our** health, **our** finances. Me, me, me.

James 4:3 is clear about this kind of thinking: 'When you ask, you do not receive, because you ask with wrong motives, that you may spend what you get on your pleasures.'

This godless teaching puts **us** at the centre of our faith. We become lords of our salvation by 'declaring' how long we will live, and how and when God will heal us and provide for us.

We require Jesus to fall into line with **our** confessions, and **our** choices.

We swap 'believe in' for 'believe for', because **believing for** puts us in charge.

In Genesis 3, Satan invited Eve to 'be like God'. He's still issuing those invitations today.

Love yourself? No!

This 'inside the camp' thinking is a perversion of Jesus' instruction in Mark 12:31: 'Love your neighbour as yourself.'

Many preachers, leaders and counsellors have flipped this command. They tell people: 'You can't love others if you don't love yourself.'

But Jesus said that self-love was a problem to be dealt with, not a quality to be nurtured.

In 2 Timothy 3:2, Paul warned that in the last days ... 'People will be **lovers of themselves.**' This wasn't an attribute.

He listed it alongside the love of money, boastfulness, pride, being abusive, disobedient to our parents, ungrateful, unholy, unloving, unforgiving, slanderous, lacking self-control, brutal, not loving the good, treacherous, rash, conceited, lovers of pleasure ...'

Self-love **causes** these things. In contrast, Jesus told us to die to self (Luke 9:23), to deny self (Matthew 16:24), and to put others first.

I've prayed for people who 'didn't love themselves'. But their self-love soon showed when I said something they didn't like.

One guy said he hated himself, but still pressured people to get his own way and jumped the coffee queue every week. His self-love was alive and well. And his 'neighbour' never got a look in.

Jesus also said in John 15:12 that we should love one another as he loved us. Fortunately, Christian psychologists find it harder to flip this command.

We will never reach our broken world with self-love because it lives like that already.

Self-love is self-centred. And it dethrones Jesus.

God's point of view

Many people feel worthless. But loving yourself is not the answer.

Healing comes from seeing yourself the way Father God sees you. He values you and loves you beyond your wildest imagination.

But you can only discover that by asking Jesus to reveal the Father, as he promised in Luke 10:22. He will.

And when he does, you will humbly change the way you see yourself.

Club Class apostles

The 12 apostles never used their faith as a bless-me self-improvement programme.

Neither did Paul.

He didn't for ask for prayer so he could buy a private jet or get rich on people's tithes. His prayer requests were entirely focused on his mission.

He asked people to pray that God would help him preach the gospel (Romans 1:8-10, Ephesians 6:19-20), that the Israelites would be saved (Romans 10:1), that he would be accepted by other believers (Romans 15:30-33), and that God would enable him to visit the people he was writing to (1 Thessalonians 3:10).

Self-love? No. He recognised that he was a wretched man (Romans 7:24), the worst sinner (1 Timothy 1:15). I wonder what counsellors would make of his 'self-image'?

In 2 Corinthians 4 he said that he was hard pressed, perplexed, struck down, abandoned, and always carried the death of Jesus in his body.

We'd probably sign him up for six months counselling. But Paul concludes by telling his friends in Corinth: 'All this is for **your benefit**.' No self-love there.

His pain - their gain.

Rebuilding prayer walls

Going outside the camp also means praying.

Jesus made prayer easy. He told his disciples: 'Go into your room, close the door and pray to your Father, who is unseen.'

Almost anyone can do that. You don't need a list, a journal or a diary. You don't need to buy a book or go on a course. You just need a room, a decision and a door.

Personally, I'll do anything to avoid prayer.

So, to make it more attractive, Jesus added: 'Then your Father, who sees what is done in secret, will reward you.'

There's a saying: 'Pray as though your life depends on it.'

But this again, is about **me**. The reality is that you and I are OK already. Our lives are hidden with Christ in God. Our destiny is sorted.

So, we must pray as though **other people's** lives depends on it. Because they do.

Broken and broke

Our country is broken after a season of God's anger. Hundreds of thousands of people are grieving loved ones. Many are sick. The NHS cannot cope.

Millions are unemployed or coping with the loss of businesses, careers, incomes and lifestyles.

It's a tragic landscape.

We are in an Isaiah 61:1 moment. Then, God's people were returning from exile, defeated and in despair. But Isaiah brought a message of hope.

In v 61:4 he said that these defeated exiles would rebuild ruined cities that had been devastated for many generations.

He was referring to cities, towns, bigger villages that were once guarded by a watchman.

And the verse refers to **many generations**, even though the Israelites were only in exile for one.

Three generations ago, most cities, towns and villages in the UK had regular prayer meetings.

Even three people praying in a church hall were enough to keep the enemy at bay.

But many churches replaced prayer with projects, music and socialising. Cynical Sanballats (Nehemiah 4:2) mocked the pray-ers, saying prayer was 'religious'.

The result? Devastation, the same as in Israel.

Devastation in Hebrew means *stunned, stupefied.* You see that on people's faces when you go out.

But now, God wants to raise up watchmen and watchwomen in every city town and village, to pray for **people.** To rebuild spiritual walls.

Cities, towns and villages aren't buildings. They are the people who live in them.

Saved souls save cities.

Many Christians believe spiritual warfare will achieve an 'open heaven' and release blessing and successful evangelism in their area.

But the anointing of the Holy Spirit opens heaven for each of us, the same as it did for Jesus (Luke 3:2).

And heaven remains open, because we can come boldly before God's throne through the blood of Jesus (Hebrews 4:16).

Heaven can't be more open than that. And no power or principality can stop us.

How to keep our love hot

The disciples once asked Jesus how they would recognise the end of the age.

He warned them about deception, tribulation and persecution. And then he said in Matthew 24:12: 'Because of the increase of wickedness, the love of **most** will grow cold.'

Most. Ouch! Maybe me. Maybe you. Most of the people in your church.

Grow cold in Greek means *to breathe and make cool.* It's gradual.

We must act now to stop it. How?

First, we need to toughen up.

Some Christians won't watch the news because they can't cope with what they see. For them, even the Antiques Road Show is a walk on the wild side.

But Jesus never shied away from the bad stuff. And he didn't have the luxury of a notice saying: 'This programme contains distressing scenes' before he went out.

He saw Romans cruelly beating women and children, people smoking hashish, gruesome crucifixions and revolting lepers.

These things didn't taint him. And watching someone being shot on the news won't taint you. Jesus said in Mark 7:15: 'Nothing **outside** a person can defile them by going into them.

'Rather, it is what comes out of a person that defiles them.'

That's true. I've met people who won't watch the news, but who happily spew lies and gossip.

Teenage rampage

When I was 17, I became news reporter in one of the roughest areas of London.

I saw the corpses of accident and fire victims, children living ankle-deep in sewage and old people dying of cold and neglect.

I sat and cried with battered crime victims, and with families whose children had been murdered, or killed in accidents.

I saw the ghastly, bloodstained wreckage of the Moorgate tube disaster and then visited 15 grieving families the next day.

I was often sick.

Looking back, God was preparing me to live outside the camp. Now, I don't like what I see, but I don't fear it or avoid it either.

Neither should you.

Look at the stains, not the windows

God wants us to look at the stains in society. His beauty is there as well as in the stained glassed windows.

We must be ready see men, women and children having sex in the streets. And where people will look terrifying, evil and dirty.

Good Samaritans walk straight towards the bloodied and bruised.

Psalm 119:37 says: 'Turn my eyes away from worthless things.' In Hebrew, *turn away* means to *pass through, to go beyond.*

It doesn't say: 'Don't look', but *don't dwell* on what you see. Don't let your eyes linger. You may weep and vomit, but then love people and pray for them

The real bigots

In 2019, police arrested a Christian preacher outside Southgate tube station in north London.

They confiscated his bible and drove him out the area. Then they dumped him without enough money to get home.

Police said his message was 'offensive', although they didn't produce any evidence or witnesses.

This was not an isolated incident. And it shows how bigoted our country has a become.

However, Christians should not complain. We are reaping what we've sown.

We are the bigots. We have been marginalising people for generations. So, now we are marginalised ourselves.

We have failed minority groups and so many others by judging them. Now, they're judging us.

Don't judge. Ever.

Our attitudes to many people have been shocking.

Believers readily quote Romans 1:26-27 to gay people, but conveniently forget to turn the page.

There, Romans 2:1 says: 'You, therefore, have no excuse, you who pass judgements on someone else, for at whatever point you judge another, you are condemning yourself, because you who pass judgement do the same things.'

Clear enough.

And yet we keep judging. Why?

Jesus stressed in Luke 6:36: 'Judge not, and you will not be judged; condemn not, and you will not be condemned; forgive, and you will be forgiven.'

It is **God's** job to judge (Isaiah 33:2, James 4:12), and the **Holy Spirit's** job to convict (John 16:8).

It's **our** job to love people, unconditionally (1 John 3:18).

Time for the good news

Jesus began his ministry with good news (Luke 4:18-19). And so, 'sinners' became his friends.

And now, as Jesus builds his church today, we must ask ourselves: 'What good news do **we** bring to people?'

Many groups, like the LBGTQ community, hate Christians because we are rude, unloving and uncaring. We judge them by their appearances and believe the worst of them.

When God listed his moral priorities in the Ten Commandments, he did not mention homosexuality. And neither did Jesus during three years' ministry.

However, he said a lot about divorce. Yet the church focuses on sexuality and gender at a time when divorce rates among Christians are around 30 per cent. This is why Christians are so often called hypocrites,

The church that Jesus built just brought good news ... a message of joy.

It's time to discover it and proclaim it.

It's too late to undo the damage. We have lost the argument, lost the battle and lost the opportunity.

So, we must pray, keep quiet, stop judging and find opportunities to show unconditional love.

The church that Jesus builds will 'go' more often than it 'stays'.

Chapter 10

A SKELETON CHURCH

Jesus has been quietly building new churches for several years. And he has used COVID-19 to lay the foundations of many more.

His 'living stones' will include thousands of people who have left UK churches during the past 40 years.

Many were recognised as men and women of God. Some were leaders or had significant ministries.

They quit because of church splits, rules and regulations, burnout, disillusionment and heavy-handed leaders.

Some were heavy-handed leaders themselves.

They are now a forgotten army of dry bones, laying in a valley. But their time is coming.

Ezekiel 37:5 says: 'This is what the Sovereign LORD says to these bones: "I will make breath enter you, and you will come to life."'

Not all of these 'revived bones' will re-join mainstream churches. Why would they?

Many will rewind to Acts 2:24 and meet as small, independent groups, the same as believers in Rome and other places on Paul's e-pistle mailing list.

Hundreds are doing that already. They are part of Father's 'ground-up' awakening described in Genesis 2:6: 'Streams **came up** from the earth and watered the whole surface of the ground.'

No more top-down, DIY no-Jesus religion.

Just streams of living water in the church that Jesus is building.

Go and get 'em!

Thousands of people have left churches and have not gone back. They need rescuing.

In the parable of the lost sheep, a shepherd left 99 sheep to search for one. Personally, I'd have cut my losses and hung on to the other 99.

But this good shepherd was different. One stray was important. And when he found it, he carried it home and held a party to celebrate.

Now, many people say this parable refers to evangelism. But if it did, it would be the parable of the lost goat. I've never understood why we apply it to non-Christians.

It refers to God's people. They are in the fold already. And it demonstrates Jesus' love and persevering commitment to find straying sheep.

That's why the shepherd left the 99. Verse 7 says they were **righteous**. They could be trusted to look after themselves.

God is weeping for his lost sheep.

And one reason we see so few souls saved is because we didn't care for those he gave us. They strayed and we didn't rescue them.

So, why would Father trust us with any others? Luke 16:10 says: 'Whoever can be trusted with very little can also be trusted with much.' We must prove we can be trusted.

Ezekiel 34:10 warns that his shepherds will have to account for every sheep. So, God will ask leaders one day about the ones who left.

It's time to start praying for our friends who have opted out of church. And search for those we lost contact with years ago.

We may need to change our priorities and leave the 99 to go and find them.

Now is the time to do it.

The church that Jesus builds will be a safe haven for people who quit manufactured churches.

Chapter 11

VISION EXPRESSED

Some people prophesied that God would give his people twenty-twenty vision in 2020.

He did. He sent COVID 19 to express his anger at our Jesus-less, DIY churches.

He showed us what he thought of career Christians who rob the poor of people's tithes.

And as for those who replaced radicalism with religion, compassion with a constitution, love with legalism, power with performance, miracles with membership, deliverance with denominations ... he closed them down, overnight.

He called time on this Babylonian-style 'Christendom' that's turned his house of prayer into a den of thieves.

Last Christmas, I heard a vicar on the news talking about COVID-19 rules, and my heart leapt as she said: 'All we can do now is put our hope in ....'

And I thought, YES! She's going to say Jesus.

But then she said: 'The vaccine.'

How tragic. If Vicars can't point people to Jesus ... well, us saints will have to do it!

Similarly, Pope Francis, Ecumenical Patriarch Bartholomew and the Archbishop of Canterbury didn't mention Jesus in their statement on climate change.

This strikes me as strange, as Colossians 1: 16-17 says: 'For in him (Jesus) all things were created, things in heaven and on earth, visible and invisible, whether thrones or dominions or rulers or authorities.

'All things were created through him and for him. He is before all things, and in him all things hold together.'

Any attempt to hold creation together without Jesus will inevitably fail.

Jesus is building his church, from the ground-up. But it will be built on self-sacrifice. And it will honour and exalt him, even if traditional leaders don't.

Kingdom when?

Some churches have proclaimed a visible 'kingdom' for many decades, and some still do. But where is it?

Show me a single city, town or village in the UK that is in a better spiritual or moral state now than it was in 1980.

The only kingdom that has expanded is the devil's. He's got a tighter grip on our nation that possibly any time in history.

And at the same time, the UK church is more secular than at any time since the Emperor Constantine.

'Kingdom teaching' is largely responsible, as it fails to properly separate God's values from those of the world. It has traded influence for affluence and conquest for compromise.

And it has produced diluted disciples who love the world rather than live like strangers passing through it (1 Peter 2:11).

Change of priorities

The kingdom of God is mentioned 108 times in the four gospels, mainly by Jesus. He only mentioned church twice.

But the focus changed after he ascended to be with his Father.

After that, the kingdom is only mentioned around 20 times. And neither the 12 apostles nor Paul ever preached about it.

In contrast, the word **church** is mentioned over 100 times.

Why? Because Jesus did not give his disciples a 'kingdom' mandate.

In fact, he didn't even mention the kingdom in any of his three final briefings. He clearly didn't see it as their priority.

In Matthew 28:19, he said: 'Therefore go and make disciples of all nations, baptising them in the name of the Father and of the Son and of the Holy Spirit, and teaching them to obey everything I have commanded you.'

No mention of the kingdom.

Similarly, he didn't mention it in Mark 16:17-18. He said: 'And these signs will accompany those who believe.

'In my name they will drive out demons; they will speak in new tongues; they will pick up snakes with their hands; and when they drink deadly poison, it will not hurt them at all; they will place their hands on sick people, and they will get well.'

No mention of the kingdom.

And he didn't mention it when he gave his 11 remaining disciples their final instructions in Acts 1. He just told them to wait in Jerusalem for the Holy Spirit.

They raised it (v6), but he brushed it aside and said it was in the **future** (v7).

145

He just told them to focus on their mission: 'But you will receive power when the Holy Spirit comes on you; and you will be my witnesses in Jerusalem, and in all Judea and Samaria, and to the ends of the earth.'

So, the apostles and the New Testament churches paid little attention to the 'kingdom' because Jesus did not ask them to.

They just followed his instructions to make disciples, and saw results that have never been matched.

If we let Jesus build his church, we will see the same.

The Kingdom is JESUS

A lot of 'kingdom' teaching is based on a misunderstanding of scripture. When Jesus told the Pharisees: 'The Kingdom of God is in your midst' in Luke 17:21, he was referring to himself, not some entity, organisation or system.

He was the kingdom, and he was right there, right then. The evidence was that he cast out demons (Luke 11:20), because he clashed with the prince of this world.

As we preach the gospel and make disciples, people's lives will be changed as they submit to the rule of king Jesus.

And then, the kingdom of God will grow, and society will change. The kingdom is the consequence, not the goal. It's lives ruled by Jesus, not a power grab for dominion on earth.

Saved souls save cities.

The future

In Chapter 1, I said that God warned me in December 2018 that he was going to send a **wave** of judgement. COVID-19 - with its first, second and third **waves** - was the result.

And then in March 2021, he told me to publish this word:

'Christians will lose their freedom unless they rapidly repent of compromise.

'If we do nothing and say nothing:

- The militant 'woke' lobby will force the government to introduce unprecedented restrictions on free speech.

- The bible will be classified as 'hate speech'.

- Churches will be required to adopt strict equality and diversity policies. Those who don't will lose their charitable status and their use of public facilities.

- Churches and Christians will be banned from social media and other online platforms.

147

- Christians will be persecuted and imprisoned for speaking biblical truths on contemporary issues.

- The true churches that Jesus builds will be forced underground.

'The Lord is giving us until the Queen dies to repent. If we don't, her death will herald a season of lawlessness and anarchy, which will change our nation permanently.

'If we still don't repent, we will be taken over by a foreign power.'

So, in the post-COVID-19 era, are you going back to normal? Back to Babylon?

Or will you join Father's ground-up awakening?

Save ME!

When COVID-19 hit the UK, thousands of 'me-first' Christians rushed to 'claim' Psalm 91's promises of protection from the pestilence and the plague.

We brushed aside the Great Commission in a stampede of 'love yourself'.

I wonder how this affected the tens of thousands of people who have died of COVID-19 in the UK?

As lockdown ends, Christians must decide whether to dash back inside our buildings to love ourselves. Or meet Jesus outside the camp.

God is shaking the system of bank-draining buildings, paid pastors, career charismatics, mercenary musicians, affluent apostles, rich revivalists, worldly worship leaders and prophets who profit.

The church that Jesus builds will be powerfully passionate, ridiculously reckless and utterly unpredictable.

It will love Jesus, love his Word and love people unconditionally. And it will be persecuted by just about everyone, especially those Christians who failed to repent of their compromises. Christendom always ends up opposing Christ.

Nothing will stop Jesus from building it. The only question is whether you and I are prepared to join in.

The church that Jesus builds has a place for *you*.

ABOUT CLELAND THOM

God healed me of an incurable back condition in 1978 and later said I would be called a prophet. I have been called many things since then!

But the Holy Spirit has somehow enabled me to bring words and insights to his church over the past 45 years.

I just provide the eyes, ears and the mouth, and he does the rest.

The results always surprise me.

Despite my fears, flaws and insecurities, Jesus has healed and delivered people, and transformed lives, situations and churches.

I now help to lead Freedom Church, a praying community that sets captives free.